DAVID CLARK was Principal Teacher of Geo
before training as a minister of religion. He se
minister in Airdrie and Dundee and in-bet
worked as the general director of Scripture
he continues to be involved in supporting theological education a
India. David is married to Maureen. They live with their Golden Retriever
dog, Ailsa, in Fife in the coastal village of St Monans. He enjoys cycling, wild
water swimming, and walking.

KATY EMSLIE-SMITH grew up in Scotland, having spent her early
childhood in mountainous Lesotho. She has worked as a general practitioner
in the city of Dundee for many years, and continues to teach medicine there.
Katy is part of the Steeple Church in Dundee where David Clark was minister
for some time. She is married with three adult children. Katy loves Scotland's
wild places and enjoys the benefits of living by the sea as a recent convert to
cold water swimming.

Landscapes
of Grace

Psalm words heard in the wildness
of Highland Scotland

David Clark and Katy Emslie-Smith

SilverWood

Published in 2022 by SilverWood Books

SilverWood Books Ltd
14 Small Street, Bristol, BS1 1DE, United Kingdom
www.silverwoodbooks.co.uk

ISBN 978-1-80042-185-1 (paperback)

British Library Cataloguing in Publication Data
A CIP catalogue record for this book is
available from the British Library

Page design and typesetting by SilverWood Books

For Maureen – journeying companion, generous in love,
an untiring encourager, and always faith-inspiring

Restore me to the rocks, where the snowflake reposes,
Though still they are sacred to freedom and love:
Yet, Caledonia, beloved are thy mountains,
Round their white summits though elements war

(Byron, *Lachin y Gair*, 1807)

Contents

Acknowledgements

The writing of Landscapes of Grace has been a collaborative work undertaken during the months of 2020-21 when restrictions on normal life were curtailed in response to the COVID pandemic. I am grateful for textual improvements suggested by Maureen Clark and Katy Emslie-Smith. I express my thanks to Alistair Emslie-Smith for his time and care in locating the photographic images that enhance the text. I have appreciated Kate Elvins' reading and commenting on the manuscript. I am especially indebted to Katy Emslie-Smith for her poetically written response to each completed chapter. Katy's writing has deeply enriched this book allowing the reader to be drawn more deeply into both the psalm writer's words and the landscapes of Highland Scotland. Landscapes of Grace is as much her book as mine. Lastly, I acknowledge the conversations over many years with many people who have shared a love for the untamed wildness of this land.

D.C.

Foreword

Perhaps it's nothing more than my weakness but I confess, I need my spiritual nourishment to come to me wrapped in layers of that which I can relate to and visualise and imagine. And as the years go by, this need increases; Lord, speak to me in ways that I can comprehend – not so much in lofty theological principles and philosophical musings but through that which is all around me and which I can reach out and touch.

It seems clear to me, therefore, that David and Katy wrote this little book with people like me in mind!

But that's not all. This book is grounded in the Scottish landscapes that I treasure so dearly. Every reflection takes me to places I've been or that are high on my list to visit. That which is described – mountain tops, steep cliffs, lonely glens, breaking Atlantic waves – stirs my soul.

And this, too, has been for me something that has deepened as the years have gone by. I venture into these wild places as I always have but now there's much more going on than the taking of physical exercise and working my way through lists of hills climbed. Now, I find that my very steps are themselves prayers and that the rocks and heather crossed over and the warm sunshine and sheets of rain experienced along the way are connections to the Creator. As never before, I'm meeting the One who made through the splendour of that which was made – and it's there the minute I step outside.

So this book embraces that which is referred to as 'outdoor spirituality' and it does it brilliantly. The writing is evocative and accessible, the prayers beautifully simple though never simplistic. But principally, it is in the weaving together of the Psalms and the often barren but always beautiful landscapes of Scotland that it excels.

Of course, the writing will work perfectly well for those who know nothing of these places but for those of us who do, it really is a gift – the devotional that we've been waiting for.

Would it be greedy for me to express a hope that Volume Two will be in the pipeline? There's certainly no shortage of material and, I hope and pray, no lack of demand as more and more we come to see what those before knew well – that God is met when the wind is in our faces and as we tramp over moor and mountain every bit as much as when seated comfortably within the confines of a church building.

Thank you, David and Katy. You've made me want to get into the Psalms more and more; to get outdoors more and more; and by combining both, to get closer and closer to God.

The Very Rev Dr Martin Fair

Taking opportunities to soak in beauty, to reflect on life's ups and downs and to consider how God interacts with us through the Bible are always worth the time we are willing to give. This book will be a great help with that quest. David weaves a tapestry that combines the rugged beauty of the Scottish Highlands in photographs and imagination with Biblical Psalms, modern poetry, and thoughtful reflections. Here is food for the soul – even if you have never visited the landscapes described. There is every possibility that you will experience 'deep calling to deep' (Psalm 42:7) as you open your heart and mind to the living God.

Elaine Duncan, Chief Executive, Scottish Bible Society.

Preface

The varied landscapes of Highland Scotland compel a more leisurely pace of travel. We leave behind the rush, the deadlines, and the task-driven demands of daily life. We become guests in a world of wildness and beauty. We draw close to crag, mountain, and river and when breathing in what's seen and heard, we allow the landscape to relate into our lives and experiences and to awaken in us a richer understanding of our journeys.

Landscapes of Grace is a book of reflections that listens to the spiritual insights of the writer of the Psalms; a writer who lived in a different place and at a different time yet who saw the rivers, the sea, the sky, and the mountain. My intention is that readers might readily connect the psalm writer's words with the landscape of Highland Scotland. My hope is that in hearing his words, readers will discover a compelling resonance with the storylines of their own journey. It is a book that seeks to encourage and affirm in times of life's uncertainties.

I am indebted to Katy Emslie-Smith for her richly poetic words which conclude each chapter. These words prompt our praise of God, as we embrace his loving presence when travelling the firm ground as well as the uneven, the gentler slopes as well as the steep, and on the days of mist and rain as well as in times of clear horizons.

As in all writing I ask for your generous understanding if I've mis-remembered a detail or even partly misunderstood some past event. My intention has been to be honest with myself and with the psalm words as I've worked at exploring their meaning in the context of the wildness of Highland Scotland.

Over many years I have appreciated the late Eugene Peterson's books on

Christian ministry. In writing Landscapes of Grace I would affirm Peterson's claim that all theology is rooted in geography.

David Clark

CHAPTER 1: An Introduction

For a few childhood summers our family holidayed in what was at that time remote Ardnamurchan. It was always the Glasgow Fair holiday. An ex-Army tent was collected and packed, and the long journey commenced – Loch Lomond, Rannoch Moor, Glencoe, and then the waiting at the ferries: first at Ballachulish, quickly followed by Corran. However, at Ardgour the journey really began, as we trundled along a tortuous single-track road to Strontian. We pressed on next to Salen and eventually to the small inlet where we would always camp, on the shores of Loch Sunart.

Loch Sunart, Ardnamurchan

I've revisited that lochside location a few times in recent years, and stopping for a moment allowed long-gone memories to return. Here, as we camped, storm clouds would march up the loch and drench us in heavy summer rain, followed by magical moments when the loch was stilled and the unrippled surface reflected the hills around.

If I can pinpoint the beginning of a love for Highland Scotland, it is here all those years ago on the shoreline of Loch Sunart. It was a completely different world, in so many ways, from the city streets of home. This beginning has led, in the years following, to a passionate appreciation of the remarkable diversity of landscapes and seascapes that shape so much of Scotland. A few years back, when conducting a communion service in Jerusalem at the end of ten great days visiting the Holy Land, I commented on the beauty of what was Jesus' homeland, but then quickly added that it still was no match for the lochs and hills of Scotland. Undoubtedly this is a personal bias, though maybe at times it is best left unsaid!

Of course, in the early years of discovering Highland Scotland, I wasn't aware of an ancient book of songs, poems and prayers that we know as the Psalms, and of their part in the spiritual formation of those living in the Highlands and Islands. I was not aware of how, for them, the long-ago words had been sung and treasured: psalm words that have brought meaning and hope to a people living among rock-strewn hills and slate-heavy skies. In some ways, the Psalms came to belong to those who lived in our glens, islands and rugged coastal fringes. I admit that my appreciation of the long-ago spoken and then, subsequently, written words has been a gradual and slow process.

Yet I should not be surprised by the Psalms' importance to the peoples of Highland Scotland. For past generations of crofters, life was extremely vulnerable and unpredictable. The harsh environment resulted often in famine, ill-health and poverty; added to this, the continual threat of eviction by distant landowners made life insecure and uncertain. The Psalms repeatedly embrace injustice, betrayal, illness and uncertainty, and yet woven into all these experiences is the assurance that God is just and will provide for his people. It should be no surprise that when history records the eviction of one Highland community from their land, it states that their final communal act as they gathered to be transported was to stand and sing in Gaelic the words of Psalm 42:

> Why, my soul, are you downcast?
> Why so disturbed within me?
> Put your hope in God, for I will yet praise him, my Saviour and my God.
> (Psalm 42:5)

As so often in the Psalms, these words bring together that remarkable mix of lament and hope of what a future day will promise. In singing the psalm, a powerless people, being exiled from home, are reappropriating truth from millennia past into their own painful experience of loss and injustice.

My interest in writing, while recognising such a powerful reappropriation of narrative, will have a slightly different focus. The strong poetic imagery used in the Psalms has for a long time connected with my imagination and my understanding of God's gifted relationship with a people. Many examples of this imagery are of landscape, seascape and skyscape. This imagery becomes so naturally revisualised in Highland Scotland that we can understand a remarkable and powerful connection between the ancient words and a people who found hope and life in singing these words in their worship.

In 1825, the final worship service of the communion season in Kilmuir (Dunvegan) in Skye was held outdoors because the people gathered numbered nearly 3000 for such a great occasion. A visitor attending wrote of the powerful final singing in Gaelic of Psalm 72:18–19:

> Praise be to the Lord God, the God of Israel,
> who alone does marvellous deeds.
> Praise be to his glorious name for ever;
> may the whole earth be filled with his glory.

He commented on how "the people seemed enfolded by the pastoral and craggy scenery around them – the heavens overhead emblematic of the residence of God whom they worship and of the final home they are taught to hope for."[i]

It is this enfolding in our hearts and minds of the visual scenery of a particular land with the imagery of a poet writing long ago that I'm hoping to explore. We cannot read far in the Psalms without coming across sky, mountain, river, seas, storm and so much more. As we revisualise this imagery in the Psalms with the familiar beauty and harshness of our land, we see more clearly how God still comes to us in our every experience and enfolds in us his unmistakable hope and purpose. More than that, as we revisualise this imagery we find given to us a remarkable hope: hope of a secure future in a final home.

But, for the present, the Psalms lead us to meet ourselves more deeply in the most rugged of times when we must demand of God his acknowledging of the anguished and passionate cry of our hearts, and when we insist that he show his goodness and demonstrate his justice.

CHAPTER 2: Awesome Sky

Geography lessons at school often involved filling in blank maps of Scotland with the names of firths, rivers, islands and towns. Sometimes a line drawn by a ruler joined Helensburgh, on the Clyde estuary, to Stonehaven on the east coast. A precisely drawn line, we were told, marked the edge of Highland Scotland. Cross that line and all becomes so different, with mountains, fast-flowing rivers, pine tree forests, lochs, bogs, ferns and heather. An hour's journey from Glasgow's urban edge would take us across that line. Not surprising that the roads to Balmaha and Aberfoyle were often travelled.

I remember a night-time walk, in my late teenage years, not far on 'the other side of that line' near the small hamlet of Kinlochard. It was then, for the first time, that I really looked at the brilliance of the night sky. It was a moment, familiar to many of us, of seeing the wonder of infinite sky and becoming uncomfortably aware of the vanity of our arrogance and seeming self-importance. Similarly, the writer of Psalm 8 looked up at the night sky and, in gazing skywards, sought value and meaning from God to redress the insignificance and brevity of human existence. He wrote:

> When I consider your heavens,
> the work of your fingers, the moon and the stars,
> which you have set in place,
> what is mankind that you are mindful of them,
> human beings that you care for them?
> You have made them a little lower than the angels
> and crowned them with glory and honour.
> (Psalm 8:3–5)

Living in urban areas, as many of us do, means that the brightness and clarity of the night sky is less often seen. The gentle glow of light pollution makes indistinct the brilliance of the distant stars. In addition, cities are crammed with buildings, shops, roads, people, traffic and more. It's enough to find our place in this created world, without spending time standing in some lonely place gazing on billions and trillions of stars. Yet, like the psalm writer, it is important that we look skyward. Certainly, a poet of more recent times, Gerard Manley Hopkins, was in little doubt of this when exclaiming: *"Look at the stars! look, look up at the skies!"*[ii]

Best, then, to travel to the Dark Sky Discovery Sites in Highland Scotland, where all can be seen: places where the sky is at its most dark – the island of Coll, Lochaber, Assynt and parts of Skye. The writer of the Psalms interprets what his eyes can see, and elsewhere, in Psalm 19:1, he affirms confidently: *The heavens declare the glory of God* – a statement about the creative magnificence of the mystery of God. But there is more – much more! He writes in Psalm 8 of how God is both mindful and caring of us and that a remarkable significance is afforded to every person's life. He writes of how each person is God-determined and that we all are crowned, purpose-given, honoured and within reach of the angels. Our world population is about 7.8 billion and we are one single digit of that enormous number, yet so significantly valued.

While walking in the glens of Highland Scotland, you occasionally come across a small patch of greener, gently sloping land, usually beside a burn. Worked and nurtured generations ago, this land provided staple crops for families now long gone. You may also find stones, nettle-edged and overgrown, still tracing the incomplete outlines of crofts that once provided sheltered homes in the wildness around. I know of such places. We can read of the harshness of those people's lives. We read of the simplicity of their lives. We read of times of hunger and times when the land refused its harvest. We read of social isolation and long, dark winters. Those who knew this as home might stand at day's end and look at the infinite night sky – when clear of cloud and mist – and question the significance of their toil and purpose. Yet we hear the words of the Psalm insisting we are crowned and honoured and purpose-given.

This issue of significance is a big challenge for us today. So many forces and pressures diminish the value and giftedness of life. We work hard at resolving such powerful influences. We work to achieve status through wealth and success. We restlessly seek to 'make dreams' that can help define 'who we are'. We cultivate large numbers of friends on social media. We can talk well of ourselves, keep busy and do many acts of kindness. We can invest our lives in our children and children's children, finding shared meaning in their stories. All of this is good and important, providing a texture for meaningful living. Yet it can all peel away so easily, leaving us threatened and unsure, and still seeking a significance that lasts. And so, to stand gazing at the night sky nudges into our minds a question: am I merely a letter in a word in a sentence on a page in a book in a library in a city in one country in this enormous universe?

Vincent van Gogh painted *The Starry Night* in June 1889. At the time he was unwell, and he would die a year later. The sky is filled with the moon, large stars and huge swirls. There's a village below and at its centre there is a church. Inevitably, art experts have provided many possible interpretative reflections. However, van Gogh explains quite simply that in the times when he felt a tremendous need for religion, he would go outside at night to paint the stars.

'Religion' is a loose word and hints at what we might do to touch or reach the One who is far beyond all that can be seen. However, if we come back to our psalm writer he invites us, in gazing upwards, to know God in all his creative majesty and power and yet God who also breathes his creative life into the untidy stumbling of our journey. God who regards us as crowned, honoured and purpose-given.

It was many years ago at Kinlochard that I really looked at the night sky. More recently, I spent time one February on the small island of Berneray in the Western Isles, a fantastic island just off North Uist. One late evening in the distant northern horizon there was a strange, lightly coloured glow, not as dramatically seen as in northern Scandinavia or Canada.

*

Aurora borealis in the northern sky

This was the distant appearing of the aurora borealis. The words 'aurora borealis' can be translated simply as 'morning light coming from the north'.

I love this because essentially the night sky is about darkness, and yet into the darkness comes an intimation of morning light at an implausible time in the night and from an improbable direction in the sky. But isn't that exactly the way of God? In his creative love, again and again he breaks into the darker stretches of our stories in ways inconceivable to the finite limits of our reasoned thoughts and imagination. Extraordinary! His unfailing love to us!

How awesome is the sky!

PRAYER

O Lord, our Lord,
The night sky stretches our yearning for you.
We survey infinity and in the darkness of space
Hear your call to pause still and wonder,
Taught by children in the art of exploring mystery.

Searching into what lies so far over and beyond us,
We hear the voice of eternity which you have set in all hearts
Ring with your invitation to humility,
As we understand our smallness in the scape of the universe
And kneel, heads bowed, humbled
Before the maker of it all.

Absent light holds the interstice between the stars
And the emptiness may chill our hearts to loneliness,
Yet as the deep indigo of night recedes
To the greening of dawn,
We see and know the intricacy of leaf and feather,
Fur and scale, the yield of field, provision of sea,
We hear again the song of love that sings
In the kindness of creation.
You come in care, loving God,
And with your finger lift our chin,
Raising our heads to receive the shared glory
Of tending your beloved world,
Crowned with the honour of this trust.

O Lord, our Lord, how majestic is your name in all the earth.

CHAPTER 3: Holy Mountain

Two hundred and eighty-two – the precise number of mountains in Scotland reaching the designated height of just over 914 metres. I've been asked on several occasions which of these mountains is my favourite, and always struggled with this question. It's not an easy choice. So many factors need to be weighed up in making my choice: the quality of view at the top; the challenge of the weather; who accompanied me on that day; and the level of adventure and difficulty involved in each journey. Too many are vying to be the favourite: Liathach, Sgùrr Alasdair, An Teallach…and many more.

Sgùrr a'Mhadaidh is one of the linked peaks on the Cuillin Ridge on

Cuillin Ridge

Skye, a spectacular, steep-sloped ridge, with sharp-edged rock and loose stone. It's suited for scrambling and requires care and sure-footedness in the narrowest of places. It was a late August day and a thick heavy sea mist had, as is often the case, shrouded the heights, giving poor visibility. Walking alone on Sgùrr a'Mhadaidh, I met a stranger. He was scrambling uphill slowly but efficiently, and we quickly found ourselves at ease continuing together. We talked as we journeyed, but never too personally except when, eventually, I asked his age, for he seemed to me well past his middle years. He willingly acknowledged he was seventy-two and then, anticipating the inevitable question 'but why are you so crazy to be wandering on these mountains alone?', he quickly added, "And I want to keep doing what is my passion to the end."

It happens occasionally that the words of another settle in us deeply and become long remembered – words we will rehear and reaccept again and again for ourselves. Continuing to do what is your passion struck me as making a lot of good sense. But a passion for hillwalking can face us with challenges and setbacks. I had a rather awkward relationship with an unimpressive Scottish hill. Beinn Fhionnlaidh is a remote mountain, awkwardly distant from Loch Affric in the heart of Scotland. It can have no claim to either beauty or rock face impressiveness. Yet for me the journey to the summit of Beinn Fhionnlaidh was often frustrated and uncompleted. Journeys can be tough and provide many challenges and setbacks; this round-topped hill eventually required seven attempts. I find the poet Norman MacCaig's words helpful, writing about hill climbing in Assynt:

> When I intrude too confidently
> it rebuffs me with a wind like a hand
> or puts in my way
> a quaking bog or loch
> where no loch should be[iii]

I suspect that, in my frequent failure to reach Beinn Fhionnlaidh, I did intrude with a casual confidence, never giving the hill its deserved respect. Time and again, it was merely a 'tag-on' summit, to be reached after completing some of the more spectacular neighbouring hills. So six times I failed, though not through MacCaig's 'wind, bog, or an unexpected loch'. Instead, I was rebuffed by energy-sapping snow, shortage of time, a companion's tiredness and even, on one occasion, by heat and drought. But the mountain had to be climbed and, on the seventh take, after sleeping overnight in the Affric woods, I was at last singularly focused in mind and heart to complete this journey.

The Judean Hills, very different from those in Highland Scotland, clearly influenced the psalm writer as he explored issues of faith and life and God. Unquestionably, the most frequent 'mountain' reference in the Psalms is to a rather unimpressive hill measuring only 765 metres high – Mount Zion. I'm afraid there would be no place for Mount Zion in the official list of Scottish mountains. However, the psalm writer invites us again and again to be pilgrims travelling to this one hill, knowing that to arrive on Mount Zion is to reach a place of encounter with God; Mount Zion is indeed a holy mountain. But the pilgrim's journey to Zion was not without its problems. Many challenges and setbacks are outlined by the psalmist, along with reasons why the journey might not be completed.

Psalm 121 is one of the great pilgrim songs collected in the Psalms and is sung on the journey to Mount Zion. Many will be familiar with the opening lines:

> I lift up my eyes to the mountains –
> where does my help come from?
> My help comes from the Lord,
> the Maker of heaven and earth.
> (Psalm 121:1–2)

Eugene Peterson suggests[iv] that the writer offers clear reasons in the verses that follow as to why the journey is tough and may not be completed: the risk of stepping on loose stone and slipping (*He will not let your foot slip* – Psalm

121:3); heat exhaustion (*The sun will not harm you by day* – Psalm 121:6); and loss of mental clarity (*nor the moon by night* – also Psalm 121:6). We can all make our own list of journeying hazards through life, and even share how we have badly fallen by the wayside on the road. For the pilgrims, God would be encountered in worship at Mount Zion, and so the journey to that hill had to be made. But extraordinarily, for the pilgrims his help and presence would also be assuredly known in every journeying threat and fear. We too get lifted up when waysided, and helped to move again in the knowledge of his accompanying grace. We sing again as wayfarers do – we sing 'alleluia', even with uncertain and trembling voices; we sing again and continue our journey.

For many of us, being in the hills is a soul-healing experience. We can stand close to corrie-etched peaks, snow-crested on a sunlit day, and we find that unusual aliveness, even after the hours of toil and exertion. Anxieties, fears and concerns are eased into a truer perspective, and an elusive peace of mind is found. And yet, good and true as this might be, the bigger story is of the journey itself. It's a journey we are invited to walk as pilgrims who increasingly find ourselves wrapped in relationship with the One who has gone before, taking his cross to a hill not far from Zion.

An old lady nearing 90, living in Lewis – McLeod was her name – put it so simply as she quoted words of a familiar hymn: "And though griefs and perplexities have furrowed my brow, if ever I loved Thee – my Jesus – 'tis now." It's that bigger story of the journey! For doing my passion to the end is no different from what Friedrich Nietzsche described as "a long obedience in the same direction"[v] – having a fixedness of mind and heart upon the One who leads us home – pilgrims who've met the One who is our help, who soothes even the most furrowed brow.

In Scotland we have a designated number of mountains, and the first person to climb them all was the Rev. A.E. Robertson in 1901,[vi] with a champagne celebration on the final peak. But let me suggest this: whether our hills are climbed or seen from the roadside, we surely must pause often to lift our eyes and celebrate the wildness of crag and rock and mountaintop!

PRAYER

Shading God,
We walk in the rhythm of our protected days –
Sunlight which kindles life, and does not burn,
Gives over to moonlight which brings rest in darkness,
And with it no fear.
Our comings and goings, seasons' ebb and flow,
Our ascents and falls, our slides and climbs
Are shielded, watched over in your care.

We know the shifting tread on shingle scree,
The uncertain slip of unfirm ground,
Yet deeper know the solid ancient rock of hills
Which shoulder us to the heights,
Lift our eyes and our hearts to the point of praise
Where what is made honours the Maker:

The God who never slumbers,
The One who helps
And the One who holds.

CHAPTER 4: Right Paths

A year or so ago, I listened attentively to a fascinating story of childhood memories. I was speaking to an older lady who lived on Skye and she was talking about her early life on the family croft. She told me that a formative influence was her great-grandmother. Often, as a young child she had to sit and keep company with her while others in the family worked outdoors on the croft. What was remarkable about her great-gran, born in the mid-nineteenth century, was that she could not read or write or speak English but she knew all the Psalms by heart in Gaelic. Reaching almost one hundred years of age, she would often sing to her great-granddaughter those long-ago words of Israel's faith. The abiding truths of the Psalms deeply heard from a woman of great age became, for this young girl, an early signpost marking out the right paths to journey through life.

Significant signposts such as these are a guiding influence on our life's journey – yet sometimes we miss them. My story of missed signposts happened long ago on a childhood holiday. A car drew up one late afternoon outside the Strontian general store in Ardnamurchan and the driver got out and asked, "How far till we reach Oban?" He had driven from near Fort William over many miles of a difficult single-track road and, even as a boy, I quickly realised the wrong road had been taken. The way to Oban? They were travelling westward to Ardnamurchan's wild edge! So what had happened? It soon became clear that miles back they had taken the Corran Ferry believing it was the ferry at Ballachulish (now a bridge), which would indeed have led them south to Oban. How could they have made such a simple mistake? How could they not have seen the clearly marked signs naming the ferry and the places the road would lead to? How could they not have read the name of the ferry on the ticket? The signposts were all there. Yet it happens; signposts can be missed or overlooked, journeys can be taken, and before long we're not where we're meant to be but instead are lost in an unfamiliar world.

Long ago the psalm writer reflected, in a very different context, on the issue of 'not being in the place we're meant to be', and made clear the real dangers involved.

> Some wandered in desert wastelands,
> finding no way to a city where they could settle.
> They were hungry and thirsty,
> and their lives ebbed away.
> Then they cried out to the Lord in their trouble,
> and he delivered them from their distress.
> He led them by a straight way
> to a city where they could settle.
> (Psalm 107:4–7)

Wandering in desert wastelands is surely indicative of personal dislocation. It is being lost in an unfriendly world, knowing no way of escape and finding no right path to take. It is knowing in oneself a disturbing aloneness pressing upon mind and spirit, which at its worst can be life-threatening. And the questioning cries are heard: 'who am I meant to be?' and 'where am I meant to be?' For I am a wanderer in the desert wastelands. Of course, easy advice, shallow and clichéd, is always readily on hand, but that can badly misguide and fail to help. For we've all known times when some might say what's needed is a change of job, time to travel, to be more yourself, strong and free and ready to embrace all things new. Others might share what works for them: retail therapy, more time for self, or making new memories to lighten the way. And 'all will be well' – but how true has that ever been? For still no healing of the soul. Still lost: a desert wanderer unsure of the way home.

*

Poor visibility on a mountain path

But in our Psalm there is a 'Godward' cry for help, and this is met with the promise of being led on a straight way to arrive at a place of habitation. In contrast to wilderness, this is a signposted path leading to a place where there is belonging, community and safety – we are no longer alone but are bound to others and centred on the worship of God. This, surely, would seem a right path to find.

We find signposts for this straight way threaded throughout the text of the Psalms, and especially so in the longest psalm of all – Psalm 119. It's a big read, but what's written repeatedly encourages us to know, meditate on and obey the statutes, commands, decrees, precepts, words and laws given to us. These 'signposts' are there at every turn, corner, twist and bend of our journey. How, then, can we fail to walk the right paths? Yet, astonishingly, after 175 verses of statutes, commands, precepts, words and decrees, the writer comments: *I have strayed like a lost sheep.*[vii] The detailed and clearly marked signposts are there, yet we stray. Lost and wandering sheep, we know, can only be helped by the most caring of shepherds.

Good shepherds are always at a premium. It's been said that a shepherd's apprenticeship can take up to forty years – nearly a lifetime. It takes so long to know the hills, to understand the vagaries of our weather, and to become knowledgeable of the sheep and their lineage. The shepherd is always learning and is frequently humbled while working with his flocks. Sheep are obstinate; they get stuck on corrie-faced cliffs; they journey on wrong paths; and they often get buried by wind-blown snow. Sheep need a shepherd, and the psalm writer makes clear that we do as well: we need a good shepherd – one whose apprenticeship was fully complete before time began, who has shaped the rivers and the hills, and who knows us in our *inmost being*.[viii] We need a good shepherd who lives every statute, command, decree and law woven seamlessly with grace and love. We need a shepherd who tirelessly and sacrificially seeks the lost, to restore them again onto right paths.

I once briefly lost a friend on the wet and thickly misted summit of Creag Meagaidh – a big lump of a mountain on the north side of Loch Laggan. He stumbled on his ankle in the mist, and I was far too focused and self-absorbed in following the path ahead to notice his absence. This was not good. There was real concern for a few hours until, thankfully, he found his way downhill. But I've since wondered if we too can become so absorbed in getting our own journey right that we fail to see those near to us who have stumbled and who might become lost.

In the past, the small crofting communities of the Highlands and islands were tightly bound in those common purposes of peat cutting, sowing and harvesting, and animal husbandry. Beliefs and values were shared and so, unsurprisingly, the setbacks of family life were embraced by all. An intuitive caring and mutual support was evident in these communities.

But today life is different and has become more fragmented, with relationships easily frayed and less cohesive. We do need a good shepherd – one who breathes his Spirit upon our lives so that we might see and stay with the lost and those who stumble, and become to them the word of grace and love. For many become wanderers in desert wastelands, seeking to find the path home.

*

PRAYER

Jesus, our shepherd,
You know our every path,
You have walked the ways of the dry desert places,
The fasted hungry wandering paths,
Where life ebbs, famined in a thirsty search
For sanctuary to settle.

Jesus, our shepherd,
You know the loneliness of the cliffside path,
Where our stumbling causes rockslide on shifting ground
And rain, mist, sleet and dark
Sever our route to safety,
For it is there that you have searched for us,
The shepherd who shoulders the risk
Of finding our way to the secure fold.

Jesus, our shepherd,
You know the green path
Where still water slows our pace
To the restoring rhythms of abundant days,
Dew, blue sky, soft grass, silken pools
Restore in the company of goodness,
As your mercy ushers us
To a house prepared
And a full table set.

Jesus, our shepherd,
You know the pain of the wounded path,
The stumbling, bloodied, burdened way,
Your weakened, wronged and driven path,
Golgotha road to a cross,
Hung in homelessness.

Jesus, our shepherd,
Gentle pathfinder making smooth our route,
Our straight, right, levelled and exalted way,
Gently guided,
Fiercely won,
Safe journey home.

CHAPTER 5: Spacious Place

Castles are very Scottish. Any calendar of Scotland will feature several. But many of our castles – Castle Tioram, Mingary Castle, Kisimul Castle, Urquhart Castle and Eilean Donan Castle – are little more than the broken ruined remains of a bygone era. This scattered castle landscape in the Highlands and Islands dates back to medieval times, when clan chieftains had hegemony over the shifting boundaries of territorial claim and ownership. These chieftains were often feuding with neighbours and were quick to engage in conflict. However, the Act of Proscription, passed in 1746[1] after the Jacobite rebellions, marked the beginning of the end to many years of lawlessness in our Highland glens. Dunvegan Castle, on Skye, is one medieval castle that has benefited from modernising and restoring. Today the castle continues as the home of the MacLeod clan chieftain. It is a major tourist attraction, with more than 150,000 people annually visiting its rooms and gardens. During the guided tour of the castle, visitors will come across what is known as the pit dungeon – a shocking reminder of medieval times. A thirteen-foot-deep hole is embedded in the rock, into which prisoners were cast and left to die. We might ask: what kind of hell must this have been – the darkness, the slow starvation, the cold, and the lack of hope of any possible escape?

Dunvegan Castle's pit dungeon illustrates what is often mentioned in the Psalms when the writer becomes distressed by the threat of being overwhelmed by the enemies around. Again and again it's clear that the destructive intention

---

1. The Hanoverian government passed the Act of Proscription after Culloden, seeking to destroy the clan system of society by banning the wearing of tartan and the keeping of weapons.

of these unidentified enemies is to cast the righteous into the pit – an outcome that will diminish or even extinguish the precious gift of life.

> I am overwhelmed with troubles
> and my life draws near to death.
> I am counted among those who go down to the pit;
> I am like one without strength.
> I am set apart with the dead,
> like the slain who lie in the grave,
> whom you remember no more,
> who are cut off from your care.
> You have put me in the lowest pit,
> in the darkest depths.
> Your wrath lies heavily on me; you have overwhelmed me with all your waves. You have taken from me my closest friends and have made me repulsive to them. I am confined and cannot escape
>
> (Psalm 88:3–8)

Psalm 88 vividly describes the pit-like existence with words and phrases such as "overwhelmed", "near death", "unremembered", "in the darkest depths", "confined" and "unable to escape". These words express how the wide reach and stretch of what we understand as meaningful life has become lessened, shortened and tightly drawn in.

We see around us today the countless ways 'the enemies' – or rather, the circumstances, abuses and unfair vulnerabilities of mind and body – can make the pit-enduring existence a travesty of the gift of life. We weep with those "in the lowest pit" and with those who inextricably are slipping down into a place where the unyielding dungeon walls leave no space and where darkness blinds all sight of light. The raw experience of this pit-like existence prompts an understandable challenge on God's supposed faithfulness – for how can the God of justice and compassion permit such blatant evil and injustice? In the

Psalms, this question of God's seeming indifference to such evil is not posed politely but rather is challenged with angry passion, by insisting on God doing what he's meant to do – implementing good and right and acting justly.

Yet woven through the difficult and darker narratives in the Psalms is the imagery of a redeeming hope. Contrasting with this pit-diminished life, an extraordinary promise is given of being rescued and brought out into a *spacious place* – a most remarkable descriptive vision of life as God means it to be. The immutable nature of God reveals to us the true enormity and extent of his commitment to 'spacious place living', and repeatedly affirms his determined stand for life against every force and power that would oppress, destroy and diminish.

The Summer Isles

He brought me out into a spacious place;
he rescued me because he delighted in me.
(Psalm 18:19)

My question would be: where in Highland Scotland would you choose your 'spacious place' to be? I would have many answers, but if only one choice had to be made it would be the view looking south over the Summer Isles from the narrow road leading to Polbain on the Coigach peninsula. The combination of the island-studded sea loch, the irregular coastline, distant mountains and largeness of sky prompt in the mind and imagination the vastness of life's reach and potential.

The 'spacious place' can be very different for others; instead of a scenic coastline view, the 'spacious place' might be known and found when resting in the flow of well-played music, sharing in the noise of a celebratory crowd or feeling deeply the colours of countryside and garden. Whatever or wherever the 'spacious place' might be, it can prompt in our hearts a new song, one that is no longer clichéd with thin words nor sung with a wearied spirit, but instead is refreshed with a true sense of freedom, vision and hope. Yet, we note, the psalm writer is quite specific when he connects an awareness of God's love – 'God who delights in us' – with 'spacious place living'. How remarkable! How extraordinary that the diminished life can find a true expansiveness and freedom when embraced by God's unconditional love.

Ultimately there is that yet-to-come 'spacious place' where all horizons stretch beyond the most creative of imaginations and where all wounds and all creased and marked lives are healed. Resurrection hope is found in the Psalms,[ix] though the references are less clearly defined when compared with the boldness of the New Testament promise given on Easter Sunday at Jesus' empty tomb. This yet-to-come 'spacious place' is our new creation when risen from the dead, we will sing:

Worthy is the Lamb, who was slain, to receive power and wealth and
wisdom and strength and honour and glory and praise!
(Revelation 5:12)

A few years ago, I conducted worship for a season with a dozen or so folk in a church near Portnalong in Skye. The church is perched on a high hillside overlooking a loch, with a southerly view to the Cuillin Ridge. Often, at the end of our worship gathering, I would stand outside and, when it was not wet and misty, I would for a moment embrace that 'spacious place' of loch, hill, rock and mountain.

Yet this stunning landscape only spreads before our eyes a glimpse of something more extraordinary – God's desire to creatively touch with wholeness and beauty our damaged and distressed lives. In fact, is it not in the preceding hour in that small hall church, in our faltering worship, that 'the pit' becomes no longer so dark and so fearful? And is it not in our hour-long, untidy and easily distracted worship that our broken and weary hearts find again a new largeness of vision? And is it not in our singing and in the silence that we discern the breaking in of glory upon the ordinariness of our everyday lives?

It is in our often inadequate worship that we are blessed in finding the 'spacious place'. And then we come to realise that with toiling hands we must look around and seek to *lift out of the slimy pit* those in their darkest need.

PRAYER

Lord, with bent backs and stiff hands,
In the hardship of winter, in the steal of death,
Robbed by thin means, and broken by lost love,
On the unyielding urban street, in the poverty of plenty,
In dark thoughts and fearful nights,
We know the belittling places, the constraints of the pit.

But time and again you lift our hearts,
In the croak and crumble of old churches,
Where strained hymns are worn threadbare
By the loved faithfulness of years,
In the skerried dance of islands
With western wave and wind,

Where the sea's horizon calls to an ache for home,
When clouds silver the blue of summer sky
And swallows stitch heaven to earth,
When candlelight comforts
In the sacred dark of night,
There you lift our hearts to the spacious place,
Where broad hope will be found in the wide mercy
Of Jesus' constraint,
His life given, diminished, extinguished
In the cold, dark place of death.

Lord, the psalmist asks is your love declared in the grave?
Are your wonders known in the place of darkness?
Your deeds known in the place of oblivion?
In the grace of the empty tomb, you answer yes
As you reach into the lowest pit, the darkest depth
And delight to bring from death, everlasting life,
Spacious, abundant, wide and free.

CHAPTER 6: River Flow

The River Orchy is a short distance river of varied character. It journeys from the edge of Rannoch Moor into Loch Tulla and onwards to Dalmally before entering Loch Awe. It's a river that is sometimes shallow, slow-flowing, with stony pools; in other parts it is narrowed by gorges, falls and rapids. It's a river of unsettled habits and stunning beauty. It's a river in which after heavy rain even the slow-flowing stretches become urgent and the bank edges barely hold the water.

Two miles south of Loch Tulla, the river sharply bends and redirects its journey through Glen Orchy. On this river bend, where the land is more even, groups of young people enjoyed holidaying for ten summers in a no-frills hostel-style building. Long summer days in the sun, rain and wind are remembered by many; days filled with games, competitions, expeditions, laughter, with each evening spent in learning about Jesus and his love for us. The unchanging flow of the river was always there to meet us as one summer followed another, always intent on its journey from the moorland heights to the waiting sea. I read recently that in New Zealand 'the river' is legally defined as having a living identity, and for me this designation has much merit. I like to think of the flow and movement of the Orchy as deserving of such an affirming status.

On one particular summer's day in the mid-1980s at this river's edge, I discerned a significant change in the direction of my life. At the river's bending it became apparent there must also come a 'bending' of our journey in a new direction of travel. On that day, God spoke. And God gave assurance that this change of course would be accompanied by his unchanging faithfulness. It was also true for others that these summer days beside the river were marked by God-given significance, and I know that this river bend of the Orchy, not far from the old humped bridge, was for many a special place, a place both of friendship and of an awareness of God. But it's only fair to add that, though a special place, it could also be an unpleasant place; on windless evenings the ferocious *culicoides impunctatus* (the highland midge) would delight to cloud around and feast on our uncovered faces, arms and legs, to our great discomfort.

The imagery of rivers and streams in the Psalms is strongly linked with the experiences and stories of God's people, and can still interpret our often stumbling journey as believers and seekers. It is at one particularly difficult time in the psalmist's life that he writes of the river:

> Deep calls to deep in the roar of your waterfalls;
> all your waves and breakers have swept over me.
>
> (Psalm 42:7)

River Orchy

In the Highlands we are familiar with this kind of fast-flowing mountain river as described by the psalmist. We can meet this river on the Orchy's journey at Eas Urchaidh (Falls of Orchy) in all its tumbling force and power. We can hear of this river in the poetic words of Robert Burns:

> Here, foaming down the skelvy rocks,
> In twisting strength I rin;
> There, high my boiling torrent smokes,
> Wild-roaring o'er a linn[xi]

But the psalm writer interprets the wild-roaring rapids and gorges as illustrative of his present situation. He is distantly separated from God's presence and is overwhelmed, crushed and powerless in the face of out-of-control life events. The 'waves and breakers sweeping over' is a potent symbol of the power of chaos, sometimes in our personal stories and sadly often in the many global tragedies of our time. For ourselves, when occasions of uninvited chaos break upon us, we long to 'kayak slalom' the turbulence of the journey, yet we find too easily we're sucked in by the flow, swept against the rocks and dragged beneath the water's surface.

For the psalm writer, 'God's distance' is geographical. God is firmly housed in his temple many distant miles to the north. Though we believe in the ever-present God, not bound by building or location, we too can find the wild out-of-control stretches of the journey to be indicative of a distant and uninterested God. We struggle to detect the nearness of God who loves and provides, when all around can disorientate us and cause fear to shadow our way.

Yet if the 'wild-roaring' stretches of the river are life-threatening then, in sharp contrast, we read elsewhere in the Psalms of the vibrant life-enhancing impact of the gentler flow of streams and rivers. The river becomes illustrative of the creative action of God bringing blessing and hope to his people at significant stages in their journey. So we meet the river that breaks out of the dry rocks in the days of Israel's forty-year wilderness journey – a life-providing river.[xii] Years later, we meet the river channelled into the city during the days of Jerusalem's siege – a life-saving river that gladdens the people.[xiii] And later again, we meet the river in the days of the homecoming from exile in Babylon, restoring the desert lands with grass and flower – a life-transforming river.[xiv] The river's flow speaks of the life-giving action of God as Spirit in the most unlikely of contexts and times: a life-enhancing river that restores, renews and revives.

Over the years, I had heard occasional references made to events in Lewis during 1949–53. Recently I stayed in an old-style bed and breakfast in Barvas, with a wonderful host who still had the weaving shed out in the back garden. Barvas is a windswept crofting township on the west side of Lewis, the homes like the beads of a necklace strung along the road running north. Barvas was the epicentre of a great spiritual revival that began in the autumn of 1949; our elderly bed and breakfast host had lived through these days as a very young woman. Here we met with a living voice from the past, who remembered an extraordinary time of 'God-awareness' on the island, when so many lives were bent in a new direction in the following of Jesus. In those special days the Psalms were sung in dance halls, in churches, in the fields, when walking on the roads, in homes and with friends. Many ordinary men and women were drawn to serve Jesus both locally and in many parts of the world. The river flow, for a season, was river-mouth wide and deep, with a life-transforming impact on Lewis and beyond.

We can look back and long for these days again. Understandable. Yet, as with 'streams in dry land' and 'rivers flowing out of rock and stone', we know the surprise of God's Spirit upon the journeys we take. Often, like the wisp of morning mist upon the land, we sense the caress of the eternal in the down-to-earthness of everyday life: in the quietness of dawn or in the freshness of the colours of spring; in the texture and shading of an artist's work or in the playfulness and smile of a child; in the love of another or in words read and heard that inspire and bless. But there is more, abundantly more – for, as with 'streams in dry land', we know the surprising blessing of the Spirit: in the hearing of the heartfelt prayer of another; in the leaping aliveness of God's ancient word; and in the sung words of praise of a gathered people. And we embrace the presence of the One who blesses and cares and loves and heals. And is it not true that if we wait and lay open our plans and hopes and dreams – God speaks?

There is a beauty in the clarity of the water in a Highland river: the varied colours of river-covered stones and the sparkling light on the surface of the flow. It is no waste of time to stop awhile and watch the waters dance and turn, and see the stillness of dark pools, and hear the flow over boulder and edge.

He leads me beside quiet waters, he refreshes my soul.

(Psalm 23:2–3)

PRAYER

Praise be for rivers!
Our thanksgiving for how their wordless metaphors
Interpret our every season, impart hope in every course and turn.
From the heights of spring melt, Mount Hermon and Mizar,
Cataracts form and fall in the tumble and race
From source to mouth, their voice heard,
Wisdom of water calling the heart
To the Fountainhead and giver of life.
As water, angry in the gorge, carves new beauty in rock,
So grace gouges promise from the hard stone of pain.
As the burn plays, in bubble and speckled pebble,
And dances light in a palette of sun and sky,
Fresh joy spumes the air, and thirsty souls restore.
The meander, slow and fertile, feeds the heavy harvest,
Enlivens the sowing, the waiting, the watching.
Estuary pushes and pulls at the hope of ocean,
Where, wide and free, waves and breakers
Shall sweep us in to a breadth of unending love,
The crystal sea.

As deep calls to deep,
God, we thank you for rivers.

CHAPTER 7: Mighty Rock

The scenery of north-west Scotland is stunning and is widely accepted as the most awe-inspiring stretch of the popular NC500 road route. The north-west's mountain-littered landscape, however, makes it awkward to link communities with any kind of 'as the crow flies' road. It is not surprising that it takes a time-consuming looping road of twenty-four miles to connect the small town of Ullapool with the village of Achiltibuie. Much of this roundabout route is single-track, with frequent stop-start passing places; it's a slow journey but scenically deserving of unrushed travel.

Back in the eighteenth century, Achiltibuie's churchgoers took a more

Ben Mór Coigach from Ardmair

direct route when walking to church at Clachan at the head of Loch Broom. Their direct route, though still measuring thousands of steps on a modern-day fitness tracker, took the people along a path beside the steep-sided Ben More Coigach – a massive lump of mountain-high rock that steeply edges the sea. Walking this path was known, challengingly, as *Taking the Rock*.

These tower-like and precipitous rock mountains of north-west Scotland consist of some of the oldest rocks in Europe and deserve to be referenced as 'rocks from the dawn of time'. Coigach itself is composed of an ancient rock type known as Torridonian sandstone, a rock type that is reddish in colour, coarse-grained and angularly layered. This is rock that over aeons of time has survived the onslaught of storm, climatic extreme, resetting of coastline, weight-crushing glacier, and earthquake. It is rock that still stands firm, unperturbed and strong, facing the wild weathering of each new day, unflinching in the face of the relentless buffeting of the Atlantic winds that blow onto our westerly shores. The Achiltibuie worshippers used to walk to church on Sundays *Taking this Rock*.

It's not surprising that the rock image is a much-used description given to the character and person of God in the Psalms: God the Rock who is unshakeable and unchanging; God who has eternally existed since before the dawn of time; God who is almighty, all-powerful and strong.

Truly my soul finds rest in God; my salvation comes from him.
Truly he is my rock and my salvation;
he is my fortress, I shall never be shaken.
How long will you assault me?
Would all of you throw me down –
this leaning wall, this tottering fence?
Surely they intend to topple me from my lofty place;
they take delight in lies.
With their mouths they bless, but in their hearts they curse.
Yes, my soul, find rest in God; my hope comes from him.

Truly he is my rock and my salvation;
he is my fortress, I will not be shaken.
My salvation and my honour depend on God;
he is my mighty rock, my refuge.
(Psalm 62:1–7)

The writer of this Psalm affirms God as *my rock*. He provides very little detail, if any, about the powerful forces that destructively seek to pull him down from what he calls the *lofty place*. How might we give content and meaning to this idea of a 'lofty place'? Doesn't the 'lofty place' consist of the good times on our journey when we enjoy an unfettered freedom to live boldly, purposefully and confidently? Doesn't it lie in the kind of life that stands tall, embracing new opportunities while realising one's aspirations and potential? However, the psalmist, because of his enemies, is on the verge of toppling from the 'lofty place', self-defining his plight pictorially as like a *leaning wall* and a *tottering fence*.

The psalm writer fears his well-ordered and confidently lived life will soon fall apart, with the rubble of what's left being a sad apology of all that God intended. It's like coming across old stone walls that once defined clear boundaries as they neatly criss-crossed our high mountains. Through time, and with neglect, they are now broken down, leaving only dispiriting piles of rubble scarring the hillside. But, in this very time of extreme vulnerability, the psalm writer can Take the Rock, claiming God as 'his rock' – his source of power and strength.

We can easily relate to 'leaning wall, tottering fence' vulnerability. Nagging guilt, the shared sorrows of others, unrelenting stress, social media angst, and so much more can storm-batter our daily journey, opening wide the deep fault lines that can so easily unsteady our lives.

We can share with the psalm writer that discomforting imbalance of the tottering fence. We can also acknowledge the longing to know again the security of the lofty place, and so be tempted to buy any quick fix remedy that's on offer. Sadly, such remedies too often are prone to disappoint. Instead, struggling with our uneasy vulnerability, we can own God as the Rock, God who is almighty and all-powerful. We can take this Rock as the solid ground on which we stand.

Geologists, of course, require a close acquaintance with rock. As regards gabbro, limestone, granite and other well-known rocks, geologists' knowledge would remain so limited if they just looked on from afar or if they only read a textbook. They must come close. It's with that closeness to the rock that they can begin to feel and see the beauty of the texture, the detailed grain, the subtlety of colour and the lichen-marked patterns.

It is the same with God the Rock, who is almighty and all-powerful. Through the remarkable story of his Son we can draw near to God's loving heart, and we see and feel most clearly the beauty and imagination of his grace and mercy and compassion. And it is as we come close to the events of his Son's passion and suffering that we meet most intimately the Father heart of God.

There is a large rock very near the heart-centre of Scotland. It's on the

Clach Cridhe

roadside, two miles short of Rannoch Station on the Glasgow to Fort William line. This rock was known as the Clach Cridhe (the Heart Stone). In the past it was an important resting place for travellers on the Road to the Isles. However, in modern times, when road builders were making a new road to Rannoch Station from Bridge of Gaur, they decided that Clach Cridhe was an awkward inconvenience, an obstacle blocking the way of the planned new road. So, without any thought to its significance, it was broken, split apart and moved aside. Today, the Clach Cridhe is called the Broken Heart Stone.

Clach Cridhe: the significance of that rock in moorland Scotland went unnoticed, and so was broken, split apart and moved aside. Is this a helpful image for us? Can it be like this that Mighty Rock is known to us?

Surely in *Taking this Rock* we meet with God who has become the great inconvenience and obstacle to the self-driven plans and pride of many.

In *Taking this Rock* we find God ever present at the roadside edge of our journey, longing to be heart-centred in our lives and story.

In *Taking this Rock* we see God torn apart, discarded, broken and abused on a cross for us.

And it's in *Taking this Rock* we learn that being ingrained in Him, there is a simpler way to live: to be high is to be low; to have is to give; to love is to serve; to live is to die.

The psalm writer, in an earlier psalm, offers a prayerful cry: *lead me to the rock that is higher than I.*[xv] Indeed, lead me to the Rock who is my strength and my salvation.

PRAYER

Lord, when time was young and red hot
Your hovering spirit created their testament,
These hills, bonded in the cooling and crushing
To peace, stillness and strength.

From ancient days
They speak of you in the voice of wilderness,
Giants who lend their brave shoulders
To the tread of those who would
Follow the hope of their faith,
Through the raised ferned valley
And on the levelled scoured hill,
The rock given and taken
By singing folk with muddied shoes
And dampened hems.

Named in respect and affection
Ben More Coigach, Cùl Mòr, Cùl Beag, Stac Pollaidh
These hills call your kindness,
Heathered hollow, gouged first,
But now moss-grown and safe,
Streams generous with green life clusters
In the rent crust of primal earthshake.
The stone of a shepherd's ring, hard hewn.

Your voice in these hills, dear Lord,
Their glory yours,
Kindness in strength,
Enduring rock, gentle Christ,
Heart centred on us, heartbroken for us.

CHAPTER 8: Disturbing Silence

In the past, the sound of lament would have been familiar to those who lived in our Highland glens. Many of our crofting communities sadly experienced repeated occasions of devastating loss: of land, home, hope and life. The people wept, and yet it seemed God did not hear their cry.

The linked valleys of the rivers Kingie and Garry, more than twenty miles long, stretch from the Rough Bounds of Knoydart to Loch Oich in the Great Glen. Over a time span of a hundred years the people of this region lost homes and land. In the aftermath of the Culloden debacle – in 1746 and the immediate years following – there were savage repercussions, resulting in the killing of men and livestock. By the early nineteenth century, the landowner was initiating forced evictions to clear the land for more profitable sheep farming. In the 1840s, the crofters who remained were devastated by hunger when harvests failed because of the potato blight. Military reprisals, enforced evictions and starvation emptied the valleys of family and community. And the people wept. In those days, in Scotland a few of the clergy ministered bluntly and wrongly, with words that spoke of these difficult times as unavoidably being according to God's will.

One warm July afternoon, I crossed the eastern end of Loch Quoich along the dam wall and then walked over into Glen Kingie. It was a perfect summer's day, yet in that lonely glen I became oddly aware of a deep and disturbing silence. I heard no sound of river, of bird, of wind or of animal. I saw no evidence of life in that gently sloping valley, though I remember seeing on the patches of better land the traced outlines of overgrown stones that once had formed neatly shaped homes in which families had lived, played and worked. On that summer day, the silence was both real and yet strangely unreal. Was it imagined? Was this silence a memorial to the sadness of a place long emptied of people and the noise of their everyday lives?

Glen Kingie

The first publication of the Psalms in Gaelic was in the late seventeenth century. Soon afterwards, they gradually became available throughout the Highlands and Islands. The genre of nearly half of all the Psalms is that of lament. It is not surprising, therefore, in these lament passages to find words angrily addressed to God for standing far off, remaining silent and forsaking.[xvi] The psalm writer repeatedly pursues an absent God with questions that demand a just response. In Psalm 13 we hear the writer's almost impolite and even irreverent challenge being made to God in that fourfold cry of *How long?*

> How long, Lord? Will you forget me forever?
> How long will you hide your face from me?
> How long must I wrestle with my thoughts
> and day after day have sorrow in my heart?

How long will my enemy triumph over me?
Look on me and answer, Lord my God.
Give light to my eyes, or I will sleep in death
(Psalm 13:1–3)

During the darker chapters of the story of Highland Scotland, such words of lament would be familiar to the people, and certainly at times would have become their own cry. How long would God's irresponsible absence last in these times of forced eviction, injustice and famine? How long would God remain uninvolved and unresponsive when so clearly his testimony has declared that justice belongs to those who are poor and oppressed?

The story is told of how Angus Sutherland, a crofter who lived in Armadale on the north coast of Scotland, suffered the loss of land and home through the infamous Highland Clearances, initiated by the Sutherlands of Dunrobin. While his house was being destroyed he led his family in the singing of Psalm 43, which would include the words: "*Why have you rejected me? Why must I go about mourning, oppressed by the enemy?*"[xvii] Remarkably, it would be through the singing of lament that the ancient words became appropriated afresh and gave voice to a family's questioning, powerlessness and anger. Yet, disturbingly, such a lament would too often be met with the silence of God. C.S. Lewis wrote that the only sound that meets the cry of the anguished and desperate prayer is "a door slammed in your face, and a sound of bolting and double bolting on the inside. After that, silence."[xviii] Was he right? How long, Lord, will you absolve yourself from the suffering and pain of your people?

How familiar are we with words of lament? Have we not all uttered *how long, Lord?* and insisted that God *look on me and answer*? Have we not all made that prayer, and yet the sky above has remained firmly closed and no answer has been heard? The silence has remained resolute. We can understand how God desires to have for himself every part of our lives, including our suffering and sadness, but surely at least he can tell us when the bad times will end. Why keep silent and condemn us to living with the unbearable loss of all hope?

In these difficult stretches of the journey, the psalm writer gives little evidence of any intentional abandoning of his belief in God. Indeed, his cry of lament is the more anguished because of his enduring awareness of an unbreakable link between God and humankind. It's true that all ideas of a faith equating with some deal-making contract with God lack credibility. The long-accepted premise of a faith paying out its quarterly dividend of well-being becomes extremely questionable. Yet the psalm writer doesn't forfeit his belief in God. Faith may seem frayed and thinly woven, but it remains indelibly stained in the grain of mind and heart. It's a faith etched within the flow and texture of the deepest part of our human story. It's a faith, as with the psalm writer, that faces the inexplicable and the hurting pains of existence, and questions God's right to silence.

My most important question must be: can lament ultimately lead to hope? Íngrid Betancourt, a Colombian politician, wrote *Even Silence has an End*, a book reflecting on nearly seven years of captivity by guerrilla militants. The words of the book's title are derived from a poem written by the Chilean poet Pablo Neruda. So does silence have an end, and can hope be found? Certainly, in the Psalms the writer rarely leaves us without words of a different song – words that are hope-inspiring.

But to hear most clearly those words of a different song, we must embrace and enter the Easter narrative of salvation. For it's on the darkest of Fridays that the Son on the Cross appropriates for himself the cry of forsakenness as written in the opening verse of Psalm 22. His cry is met with God's absence and silence: a closed sky that stretches through the hours of Friday and all day Saturday. Yet with sunrise on Sunday comes that different song, with large words that promise resurrection, renewal and re-creation. Easter portrays powerfully the loving action of God. God acts out his Word for us through his pain and suffering, and by hearing this we appropriate through faith his hope for our lives.

My question was: can lament ultimately lead to hope? We would not speak in platitudes, nor do we offer words of little substance. We journey with one another, often speaking sparingly, but doing so as humble prophets of both the mysteries of life and the ineffability of God. Because of what we know from and read in his Word, and from what we have seen in his Son, we must live the promise that every silence has its end.

A long time ago, I enjoyed a solo camping expedition in the Glen Affric area of Highland Scotland. It lasted four days and, surprisingly, I met no one. At the end of the expedition, I confess, I longed to meet one other person who would break the silence of my isolation. I walked out of Affric on a mountainside path to the Cluanie Inn road, eagerly looking forward to crossing paths with someone who would bring an end to my days of silence.

What if we are to be that 'silence ending' for others: the 'silence ending' for those who long to hear God speak his word to them again? What if almost inaudibly, yet distinctly, there can be heard in us his *still small voice*?[xix] What if the authenticity of this voice is not heard through our skilful choosing of kindly words but is heard most deeply through our own brokenness, loss and fear? And what if this voice brings the words and melody of that different song: the promise of resurrection, renewal and re-creation?

For every silence has its end.

PRAYER

Lord, our land still holds the sadness
Of those who were cleared from home and field.
We smell the sorrow in the stain of cut peat
And hear the curlew's call, low over brown land,
A seeking song, bereft.

Their lament would raise to you the psalmist's questions
In loss and pain, "How long, Lord?"
Their call to a seeming faceless God for answer
Echoing back into the silence of an emptying glen.

Lord, for our world we share their lament,
The wrestled thoughts of your absence or forgetfulness.
Yet might silence allow for a deeper listening?
Might the wait of suffering bring a testing
Of how love meets with the depths of pain?
Might our wondering take us before a thirsty Christ,
Hung by nails, with a hole in his side, waiting,
Asking if he too was forsaken?

And might the searching songs of anger and grief
Find the refrain which kindles our frail hope,
Allows us to dare to believe in unfailing love?
"He is risen."
On a morning of new mercies
The silence is broken.

CHAPTER 9: Resounding Sea

There are many end-of-the-road places in Scotland, and one typical example is Kilmory, on Ardnamurchan's north coast. A small community, set on a very minor road, it's not far from the township of Kilchoan. On visiting Kilmory, no one can fail to appreciate the stunning views looking north to the varied islands of Muck, Eigg and Rhum. It has a beautiful setting. However, like many other remote places in Highland Scotland, most of Kilmory's homes now belong to holiday residents, with only a very few occupied permanently. It's that so-familiar story of decline, with school, church, post office and shop all long closed.

One Sunday in August 1840, a young minister still in his twenties arrived at Kilmory to conduct worship. The people had already gathered and were praising God in the singing of the Psalms. Later, the minister wrote in his journal: "Before I went into church I sat down on a knoll to gaze on the scenery. I heard the sound of praise rising from the primitive edifice, and the lash of the waves of the great Atlantic on the shore, and between the hymns and the ocean and the majestic scenery around there was a perfect oneness. They all praised God."[xx]

His reminiscence interlaces sounds, sights and song in describing an expansiveness of praise to God. His words easily resonate with the Psalms, as so often their ancient words boldly declare creation's praise to the glory of God. The writer of Psalm 96 describes this 'perfect oneness' of cosmic praise and invites the singing of a *new song*, a song that thrills with a fresh awareness of God's greatness and goodness.

Sing to the Lord a new song;
sing to the Lord, all the earth.

Let the heavens rejoice, let the earth be glad;
    let the sea resound, and all that is in it.
Let the fields be jubilant, and everything in them;
    let all the trees of the forest sing for joy.
Let all creation rejoice before the Lord, for he comes,
        he comes to judge the earth.
    He will judge the world in righteousness
        and the peoples in his faithfulness.
            (Psalm 96:1, 11–13)

Let the sea resound in exuberant joy to the praise of the Lord, for he has come to reign over all and set right the world with his justice and peace.

West coast, Berneray

Let the sea resound as most surely it does whenever we stand on our unsheltered coastlines, on islands Tiree, Berneray and Harris, or on a mainland edge, such as Sandwood Bay. We see and hear the 'lash of the waves on the shore': roaring noise and crashing breakers and white-foamed surf. The sea, uninhibited in its wildness, churns and twists with ceaseless energy and with a restless beauty as it breaks upon the shore in patterns unfixed, celebrating the glory of God.

And like the resounding sea we worship God with the leaping wonder of our dance, and we celebrate his reign and intention to make all things new. We praise our God as he brings his justice and equity to reset and restore our self-bent lives and our scarred and damaged world.

Yet it's easy to linger, like the visiting minister at Kilmory, on that small rising of ground outside the church and be awe-filled by the beauty and wildness of creation's song. If not lingering at the sea's edge, then it's easy to stay awhile on some high mountain or upon a rugged cliff edge, or gaze on the tumbling water of a fast-flowing river, and be moved in spirit by the grandeur and beauty of creation around. Unquestionably, the wonder of nature restores and heals. Yet our praise of nature's beauty is not quite synonymous with that long-ago command, stone-written, insisting we bow the knee exclusively before the Creator God.[xxi]

Obedience calls us to leave the sea's edge and the mountain height and labour in that strange work of creating community: a purposeful and spiritual community tasked with the praising of God. Of course, this is far from straightforward, and yet, for as long as we can remember, people have made their journey to unadorned halls, buildings with steeples and the grandest of cathedrals and, as communities of faith, have bowed the knee in their praise of God. The Psalms uncompromisingly remind us that we belong as part of an 'assembly' that gathers around the 'sanctuary' within a 'temple' to celebrate the wide stretch of God's love and mercy. There can be no opting out, no journeying alone, no avoiding being part of this 'hallelujah chorus' to the One who is Creator, Redeemer and Lord.

But help is needed with this task. We need help, for too often we struggle with a dullness of spirit and a heaviness of heart that leaves our praise listless and unfelt. At times we come to the temple besieged by the invasiveness of life's distractions, knowing well their capacity to slide shut any glimpse of the splendour and mystery of God. For millennia, help has been generously offered through the diverse traditions of church practice. We've accumulated a dizzying array of religious accoutrements to aid and enable our worship: rituals, festivals, actions, special words, furnishings, pictures, holy clothing, liturgies, music and song. All are prefixed as sacred, and yet of their real worth and true value we remain somewhat sceptical and unsure. Of one thing we are certain: with such a smorgasbord of ritual and symbol, we must train and set apart a priesthood – a specialist people who are expert in all things God-related, who can guide, manage and facilitate our God-pleasing praise.

Yet the difficulties still abound. The priesthood, with their responsibility and power, can become abusively controlling; the sermons too often become vacuous; the rituals and actions easily become fatigued in their familiarity; and the songs, music and building become more loved than the God we worship. Do we simply concede and accept that worship can only be the faintest imprint of heaven's praise? Do we settle for becoming tourists of the sacred, no longer remotely sensitive to the wonder and glory? Do we become so practised in trivialising our worship that we have little expectation of awe-filled encounters with the majesty of Holy God?

Annie Dillard pointedly writes of attending church on Sundays – "Does anyone have the foggiest idea what sort of power we so blithely invoke? … It is a madness to wear ladies' straw hats and velvet hats to church; we should all be wearing crash helmets … they should lash us to our pews. For the sleeping god may wake someday and take offence or the waking god may draw us out to whence we can never return."[xxii]

Creation seems untroubled by the deficiencies and difficulties we experience in doing worship. The psalm writer describes the wild praise of the 'highest heavens', the 'resounding seas', the 'joyful singing forests' and the 'harvest and livestock filled fields'. Creation knows the awful and awesome majesty of the

One who, in thunder and fire and in the brilliance of light, bang and explosion, creates and makes and sustains. Creation knows with what sort of power our God reigns and so, with unleashed energy and joy, creation's song is heard!

But here is the great miracle. As we gather Sunday by Sunday, the Spirit of God moves among us. We come to our halls, auditoriums and churches and are reminded that we are bound by the Spirit as 'the body of Christ'. What a remarkable privilege. We come and, by word and song, the Spirit affirms anew that we are loved and forgiven. We come and the Spirit brings delight in singing afresh the songs of the unchanging truths of grace and mercy. We come and the breath of the Spirit compels us to own the life of Jesus and to receive from him a passion for the weak, the poor and the lost. We come Sunday by Sunday, often wearied and heavy burdened, and the Spirit lifts and holds and we have rest. Is not all of this the miracle of God with us?

As I listened recently to a friend describe her story of worship, I could not fail to hear and see something of the 'resounding sea'. Brought up in Skye, she described the singing of the Psalms in her church each Sunday as being like a "full-body experience" – completely given over to being drawn close to God within the swell of the oneness of the voices around and in the firm grasp of the truths of the words sung. Like the 'resounding sea', high reaching, its rise and fall and the strong waves moving ever forward with every part held as one – so too is our worship as his Spirit moves. Hallelujah!

PRAYER

Lord, every day a new song,
The joy of a glad earth in a rejoicing universe.
Forests and fields will make harmony
With the pounding and resounding of the sea,
Beating the rhythms of praise,
Splendour and majesty, strength and glory
In all the earth, your sanctuary.

We catch the refrain
And contain it in our thin hymns,
Sung inside walls painted too long ago,
A thready melody, no match
For the thunderous wild worship
Of fire and ice, sunlight, wave, wind,
Silvery shore, dark sky.

And yet, Lord, you invite our offering,
And gather us to your courts;
Your holiness draws near,
In love that makes the unlovely beautiful.
The universe pulses glory,
And with all the earth we bow the knee,
Sing our new songs,
And tremble.

CHAPTER 10: Parched Land

The Psalms are amazing in the way they consistently explore real-life insights into a faith relationship with God. Yet we rightly handle these with great sensitivity, knowing how these songs belong within a community defined by its unique history, interpreted through the experience of God's grace and leading, which binds a people inseparably to a land that was long promised. At times it almost seems as if the psalm writer's words of praise and prayer are held, caressed and shaped by that land with all its shade and colour, its sparsity and plenty, its valleys and high places.

The Holy Land, to which the Psalms originally belonged, has many varied landscapes, but two in particular have a special significance. The annual 200-millimetre isohyet[2] is the critical boundary line between these two distinct landscapes. On one side of the line is a land of potential abundance, with pasture, timber, vine growing and crops. Life here can be settled and secure. However, cross that line and journey south or east of Jerusalem and we quickly enter a very different world of diminishing rainfall. Life becomes increasingly sparse, fragile and uncertain. This is the parched land of wilderness, a landscape with its seasonal rivers and absence of vegetation. These two sharply contrasting landscapes epitomise a tension at play in the story of God's people as well as in the story of all our lives: the interplay between abundance and scarcity, between hope and despair, and between living and dying.

The Psalms never permit us to forget the parched land wilderness, with

---

2. An isohyet is a line on a map that connects points that have the same amount of rainfall in a given time period.

reminiscences of how once the people had travelled for forty years through these desert places.[xxiii] Challenging and testing times. Other psalms clearly had a desert origin, especially those ascribed to a time when David was hunted by Saul and made his home for nearly ten long years in dry and barren places.[xxiv]

'Parched land' is not a description we can readily apply to Scotland's Highlands. But I remember, during the hot dry summer of 1976, staying briefly at the Inveroran Hotel, near Bridge of Orchy, when the water supply had become so scarce that we were directed to the nearby loch if we needed a bath or a shower. Yet even though some small rivers and burns had dried up, and the peat had become crusty-hard and the grasses somewhat yellowed, there can be no obvious equivalence between our land and the deserts of the Middle East.

But interestingly, Frank Fraser Darling, the famed ecologist, coined the phrase "wet desert"[xxv] as a suitable description for large parts of the Scottish Highlands. With the 2000-millimetre isohyet looping around our Highlands, no one can quibble about the usage of 'wet', but I suspect we might question the appropriateness of referring to our mountain areas as a 'desert' landscape. However, Darling argued, over half a century ago, that our Highlands had deteriorated into an impoverished landscape. A land that once provided a rich diversity of life had now become depleted, less biodiverse, and no longer life-sustaining for many species of plant and wildlife. It is a dying land, not as a result of drought and heat but as a consequence of greed and poor land management.

This life-diminishing impact on our environment is a familiar story: the overgrazing of sheep; the excessively high deer population; the scarring of hillsides by an enormous increase in the numbers of walkers and hikers; the vast areas of regimented Sitka spruce plantations; the popularity of wild camping and the overcrowding of 'must visit' tourist locations; and the greater intensity of damaging moorland wildfires. Increasingly we have transformed our mountain landscape into large tracts of barren wet desert.

All of this, causes great concern and prompts an urgent response. We need a healing in our relationship with the created world. One disturbing outcome of the decline in biodiversity impacts on Christian theology. We are familiar with many of the essential attributes of God: holy, powerful, creator, healer, saviour, and love. But we can often overlook the characteristic of God's beauty – *to gaze on the beauty of the Lord.*[xxvi] This beauty is not only a temple experience but one that is glimpsed, in all its richness, in creation – in the vast paint-filled palette of colour of sea, river, plant and land. Lose that wealth of diversity and we deplete our imaginative capacity to behold the greater beauty – the beauty of the One who creates all life.

However, loss of biodiversity has not been such a serious issue in the deserts of Ziph, En Gedi and Sinai. These parched lands, largely unchanged, stretch back aeons to long before any footprint pressed upon their wind-blown sand and dust. The deserts, with their sun-bleached bones, angular rocks and dried-up valleys, became for biblical writers an illustrative statement of God's absence. In Psalm 63 we meet David in this God-forsaken wilderness, crying out in prayer:

> You, God, are my God,
> earnestly I seek you;
> I thirst for you,
> my whole being longs for you,
> in a dry and parched land
> where there is no water.
> (Psalm 63:1)

Threatened by civil war, the wilderness mirrors David's state of mind as he strives to make sense of all that has happened. His only hope is God, a sentiment he makes clear in a later psalm as he prays: *I spread out my hands to you; I thirst for you like a parched land.*[xxvii] And God hears and God is there. In the dry, inhospitable, life-diminishing wilderness – God is there!

*

68

Fisherfield wilderness

In our times, what would we identify as life-diminishing wilderness? The prison cell, the dry Sahel, the wartorn city, beside the poor in our streets, among the stateless in refugee camps, and in the desolation of personal loss – God is there!

I once enjoyed spending two beautiful days in May walking in the Fisherfield Wilderness, sometimes known as the Great Wilderness. An Teallach's rock-thrusting heights towered over the path leading to Shenavall and onward into the wilderness beyond. This 400-square-kilometre area lies between Loch Maree and Loch Broom: barren, bog-littered, scree-sloped and treeless. It is a vast desert of emptiness.

Leaving aside the empty landscape of north-west Scotland, what of our cultural landscape? Its many attractions have progressively facilitated an invasive amnesia of God and of all things holy and sacred: a desert of emptiness. We may loudly promote the diversity of all life and yet become blind to the beauty of God in our lives. Long-held truths, ideas and principles are defaced and devalued. And poetic words from a different time stir the memory and can resonate today: "Hollow men […] Shape without form, shade without colour […] gesture without motion […] This is the dead land/This is cactus land".[xxviii] But is all this too harsh an indictment? Is this not a careless denial of the obvious good seen in our contemporary cultural landscape? Possibly; but occasionally we need to be disturbed if we are to hear and understand the beneath-the-surface cry of so many. There is an emptiness, a loneliness, a cynicism, an anxiety, a doubt in self-worth, which finds plentiful space in a person's heart. We need bold, easy-to-read signs warning that the parched lands of God's absence are not where life is found.

Yet we remember, in our psalm, David prayed and cried, *I thirst*. God heard and God was there! And God, who once led his people to a promised land, will still lead us home through the wilderness lands.

PRAYER

Our God, forgive us.
Forgive us for the ways in which we have
Demanded what we crave from you, our provider,
And from the earth, our cradle and protector.
In our quest for more, we have famished our wanting,
We have taken your gifts of abundance
And created the poverty of too much.
We have said enough is not enough.

We have made others thirsty
In the dry lands where the wind whips over hot soil,
Crops fail, sun scorches, fires burn.
Yet, God, you are merciful.
You have promised the shade of your wings
In the fierce heat of parched land,
Where water will flow from the split rock,
The desert will turn to pools and springs,

70

Cedar, acacia, olive and myrtle will grow,
Pines, fir and cypress,
A myriad of greens, the colouring in
Of the habitat of your glory.

Lord, in all our droughts and famines,
We remember you, our Rock and our Redeemer,
In your mercy come,
With manna and rain,
Enough for those who want,
Enough for those who need.

CHAPTER 11: Abundant Harvest

The total land mass of the Highlands and Islands amounts to more than 25,000 square kilometres, for the most part comprising rugged land of rock, mountain and steep slope. This measured area is not large, being one-third that of Ireland and slightly less than the size of Belgium. Harvesting this area profitably has been a repeated challenge over the last 250 years. An unsympathetic climate, conjoined with thin and often waterlogged soil, has mitigated against successful agriculture. There have been many attempts to improve some of the better land but these have often been unrewarding, despite much toil and struggle.

Yet harvesting from this land and its coastal edge has been possible and at times has been profitably achieved in a variety of ways:

- The late eighteenth century onwards: **sheep** (na caoraich mor[3]) were introduced in large numbers to hill areas, bringing profit to landowners but at the cost of removing many crofting smallholders from the land.

- The early nineteenth century: **kelp** (seaweed) has been processed by crofters for industrial purposes to the neglect of their own land, with most of the profit being enjoyed by the landowners.

- The late nineteenth century: **sporting estates** proliferated

---

3. 'Na caoraich mhòr' ('the big sheep') was what the Highlanders called the imported blackface and Cheviot stocks, distinguishing them from their own smaller breeds.

throughout the Highlands, bringing some local employment as well as conflicting tensions over land use.

- The 1920s onwards: **forestry** became an important source of timber, providing a reliable source of employment for some, although the large-scale planting of quick-growing Sitka spruce has not enhanced the scenic value of our mountain landscape.

- The 1940s onwards: **electricity**, through the construction of more than fifty hydroelectric power schemes, has brought an enormous benefit to industry and to the quality of people's lives. However, it has left our landscape scarred and ugly, with unattractive concrete dams, buildings and pylons, and a sterile apron of gravel and stone edging on many of the enlarged lochs' shorelines.

- The 1960s onwards: **people**, in increasing numbers, have been visiting Highland Scotland from every part of the world to experience our castles, waterfalls and viewpoints. Visitors support the local economy, yet they also overwhelm the well-known places of beauty and interest (such as the Old Man of Storr and Quiraing in Trotternish, Skye[4]).

---

4. By 2016 more than 150,000 people walked to the Old Man of Storr and around the Quiraing annually. This is typical of the people pressure on many places of beauty in Scotland. A Highland Council Tourism Committee report (17 March 2021) now indicates an estimated 200,000 visitors annually.

Old Man of Storr, Skye

This brief and rather hurried journey, illustrating the harvesting of our land, is undoubtedly simplistic. Additionally, it is not attempting to provide a definitive list of economic initiatives made over the last two centuries. But sheep, seaweed, deer and grouse, planted trees, flowing water, and visitors have all brought a measure of economic benefit and progress. The difficulty has been that these very varied harvests have been both limited in impact and very mixed in their blessing.

It's very easy to be critical of the past, but too often the land has been narrowly valued as a useful commodity: a bountiful resource to be exploited for our economic gain. Justification of such an approach can always be made by appealing to the beneficial outcomes that will surely be enjoyed by the community. But, sadly, far less is heard of the concerns of an unhelpful commercialisation and of the long-lasting impact on our environment.

These harvest seasons have often rewarded the few instead of the many and have been achieved or reaped without a sensitivity to the many interrelationships between culture, landscape and natural life. John Muir succinctly reminds us of the role of interconnectedness in valuing and understanding the natural world in his frequently quoted statement: "When we try to pick out anything by itself, we find it hitched to everything else."[xxix] And over the last two centuries, too often in the harvesting of our land we have 'picked out', with scant awareness of how all things are hitched together. Our varied harvests have become a story of mixed blessing.

However, the psalm writer, in his reflection on harvest, emphasises an even greater interconnectedness that needs to be appreciated if we are to understand and value our land. His insight is immensely significant! His words are taken from Psalm 65:

> You [God] care for the land and water it;
> you enrich it abundantly.
> The streams of God are filled with water
> to provide the people with grain,
> for so you have ordained it.
> You drench its furrows and level its ridges;
> you soften it with showers and bless its crops.
> You crown the year with your bounty,
> and your carts overflow with abundance.
> The grasslands of the wilderness overflow;
> the hills are clothed with gladness.
> The meadows are covered with flocks
> and the valleys are mantled with grain;
> they shout for joy and sing.
> (Psalm 65:9–13)

The psalm writer is convinced that, on completing the work of creation, God did not retire into a long, inactive seventh day of rest. Instead, God continues to work creatively through his caring, enriching, providing, softening, ordaining and blessing. And these actions of God are written deeply into the harvest story, challenging us to consider a better way of engaging with our created world. A new mindset is needed. We cannot any longer commodify the natural world, assuming we are entitled to 'take from' the land and reap short-term economic gain. Instead, we must ponder and reflect on how to align ourselves with the Creator God, ever aware of the creating Spirit renewing and remaking in the drama of wind and rain, soil and rock, and sea, sky and land. It is then we realise that all is gift. Nothing of the harvest is ours by right. We work and serve, knowing all things are 'hitched to everything else' but also recognising that 'all things' are sustained and owned by the One who made the heavens and the earth in their vast array.

But there is more to this psalm, and we must permit all the writer's words to be heard. For when we read the opening few verses,[xxx] we are prompted to reflect on the high valuation given to each of our lives. The harvest, the psalmist makes clear, is not just applicable to the 'meadows', 'hills' and 'valleys'; it is also the testimony of our own journey. God's intent is to shape the soil and slope of each of our lives and to work creatively: responding, forgiving, choosing, blessing and filling with good things. Of course, we must participate and realign ourselves with God by embracing the life of faith, obedience and worship. The harvest fruit, as on the land, is exceptionally good: *Things like affection for others, exuberance about life, serenity. We develop a willingness to stick with things, a sense of compassion in the heart, and a conviction that a basic holiness permeates things and people. We find ourselves in loyal commitments, not needing to force our way in life, able to marshal and direct our energies wisely.*[xxxi]

Harvests are often measured in tonnes per hectare. Thank goodness we have no equivalent assessing of the harvest outcome of our own lives! However, we must take account of one characteristic that is so contributive to an abundant harvest. Older people in the Western Isles make mention of this characteristic when speaking in Gaelic of the *miann* (an ardent desire, with reference to God).[xxxii] It's an all-defining longing that thoroughly permeates all our life: the shadows, the memories, the hopes, the decisions, and both the present and the future. In religion there is much that can be faked, but the *miann* can neither be contrived nor cheaply bought. It requires the deep soil of our lives to be creatively worked: the ploughing, harrowing, fertilising, levelling, and rock removing – especially the rock removing – and more!

This is often unsettling; progress is easily thwarted by a deep-seated spirit of resistance. Yet we must allow this work – even welcome and receive this work in our lives – so that the intensity and beauty of *miann* might bless the way we live, who we are, how we act, how we love and how we die. There are no short cuts. There is no five-step course in an easy-to-read manual promising to make this happen. But, in the words of the psalm writer, we will then journey home while 'our carts overflow with abundance'. And we will *'shout for joy and sing'* with ever-lasting gratitude knowing all is gift from beginning to end.

PRAYER

Lord, we recognise our trampling transgressions,
Our land overgrazed and stripped,
Monocultured, drained and droughted,
Soil and air exhausted
In the greed of demand for yield.
So too in the fields of our own lives.
We are overwhelmed.

Yet for this you have atoned.
With hope for all the ends of the earth
And the farthest seas,
You come, the patient sower,
In seasons' rhythm,
Seeding in all kinds of hardened land,
Caring, enriching, drenching, softening,
An abundant harvest, the crown and mantle
Of your loved earth.

Lord, where morning dawns and evening fades,
In our measured days, may we find our own harvest
Grown in your Spirit's gentle work of power,
Green shoots of new compassion,
Seasonal rhythms of patient faithfulness,
Disciplined furrow of self-control,
Blossomed peace, delight in this gifted life.

Healed to our world, restored to connect,
May we sing the joyful songs that you call out
In the overflowing blessing
Of harvest home.

CHAPTER 12: Daybreak

Singing in the shower or when driving in the car or singing with others at the back of the bus might not be too surprising, but far more unusual would be singing in the early hours of the morning in the darkness of a cave while hiding from your enemies. Our psalm describes such a moment in David's life.

Quite often a psalm has a prefixed title describing briefly the historical background providing the contextual synopsis of the words that follow. Psalm 57 is such a psalm, identifying itself with an extremely difficult time in David's story. A paranoid king is intent on destroying him and, with the help of the king's son, David wisely flees the royal court, leaving behind all the status and privilege of his successful young life. Fear of the king's soldiers and the Philistines leads David to hide in a cave: a dark place, possibly well concealed and difficult to access, but providing a place of refuge.

Caves are everywhere in Scotland, and one cave I especially remember is found on the south coast of the small island of Eigg. I holidayed with some friends on this island nearly forty years ago, staying in a damp cottage not too far from the pier – a cottage that enjoyed a spectacular view over the whole length of the Ardnamurchan peninsula. We quickly discovered that there was actually not very much to do on Eigg, other than climb An Sgùrr (400 metres high), which for one of us became the daily challenge. The highlight of the week was the CalMac ferry's arrival on the Wednesday. We all gathered at the pier to collect parcels and food and be assured, so it seemed, that island isolation need not completely disconnect us from that larger world of mainland towns, shops, cars and people.

But what of the cave? In the days of clan warfare in the late sixteenth century, the story is told of how most of the population of Eigg had to flee into Uamh Fhraing (Cave of Francis). Caves are places for those not wanting to be found. The MacLeods of Skye were arriving to exact vengeance on all MacDonald islanders for a past demeanour, as these were brutal times of tribal warfare. Though the cave is well concealed, sadly the people were found and no mercy was shown. Of course, it is hard to verify the truthfulness of this massacre, but the story is told and old bones have been found. Caves in Scotland have indeed been places of refuge, but equally – and sadly – they can become places of imprisonment, capture and even death.

Caves are breakpoints where the surface landscape is pierced and an inner world is reached. We cautiously tread into these dark recesses. But that inner world, for David, became a transformative experience in his story. So easily the cave could have imprisoned David, who may have been overwhelmed by his grievance and by the fear of what lay ahead. The skyless darkness of where he hid would have matched the dispiriting shadows cast upon his uncertain future. Staying in that cave for too long would most certainly have led to his capture and death, but instead we read of a remarkable reawakening: his renewed enthusiasm for his God-promised destiny as the righteous leader of Israel.

My heart, O God, is steadfast,
my heart is steadfast;
I will sing and make music.
Awake, my soul!
Awake, harp and lyre!
I will awaken the dawn.
(Psalm 57:7–8)

These words boldly intimate the change in David's life: *I will sing and make music … I will awaken the dawn*! He sings exuberant praise in the sanctuary of a dark cave, knowing God as the One who is ahead, behind and beside in every discomforting transition to be faced.

To sing praise to God is soul-refreshing. Until recent times, people's worship in the Western Isles centred on the Gaelic psalmody, with the precentor 'putting out the line'. In a large worship gathering there could be an astonishing number and variety of grace notes embellishing the praise. This would transform the frequently sung words into a new song, with every singer doing their own thing and expressing their own feelings. Unique! When singing the Psalms, people's inhibitions are diminished, the cares of the world are eased and the spirit is re-energised for the days that lie ahead.

A Highland dawn

We have no idea what David's solo singing and making music was like as it echoed around the cave, but his God-centred worship overcame his fears and renewed his spirit with a new impetus to live and serve. Enough of the night and the darkened gloom of the cave: *I will awaken the dawn!*

Have you a special memory of a time and place while watching the gradual arriving of a new day? That first trace of softest light in the eastern sky, followed quickly by a surging glow of colour as the dark is dispelled. And then we see, on the distant horizon, the red-gold curved edge of the rising sun – it's happening: daybreak has come. Every sunrise is a unique work of art in the texture of colour and shade of light – the stunning beauty of the new day now that the night is over. David seeks to drag into the darkness of his night the light of daybreak, determined to live with hope and intent, embracing the promise of God's sending love and faithfulness. David's new day is a unique work of God's Spirit; but then equally, in the tangled complexities of our own stories, we too recognise similar unique Spirit-blessed occasions and their lasting influence on our lives.

Shortly afterwards David's cave hiding would end, not with the arrival of the king's soldiers but instead with the coming of help and support from family and several hundred others ready to share in his journey ahead.[xxxiii] It's an important reminder of how God *sends* his love and faithfulness, reaching us in ways that are tangible, practical, unexpected and yet well timed.

Fifty years later, when reflecting back over his life, David acknowledges important principles of leadership, one of which he describes as being *like the light of morning at sunrise on a cloudless morning*.[xxxiv] What an interesting comment. His long-ago 'daybreak' moment in the cave had defined the way he lived and how he exercised his kingly rule. Of course, he failed often, yet he underscores how the transformative experience of the cave had become patterned in his life as he sought to effect 'daybreak' in the lives of others, bringing about new beginnings, new hope and new possibilities.

'Daybreak' moments are many and varied and do not necessitate a dark cave setting. I've listened to others over the years tell their stories and share their 'daybreak' moments. The settings have varied: the small Spanish village; the London street; the hospital bed; while walking in Edinburgh; the snowfields of northern Norway; while sitting in a church; through seeing a vision; while reading a book; and even when parachuting over central Russia. How extraordinarily unique are the circumstances and places where the grace of God is found and seen. The resourcefulness of the Holy Spirit is limitless. Yet for others, 'daybreak' moments have not been so obvious, and only with the passing years have half-forgotten words and encounters, dormant and unwrapped, finally been heard deeply and their defining influence realised.

I once walked, as through a door, into a new 'daybreak'. It seemed very much that way to me. Leaving Morvich beside Loch Duich on Scotland's west coast, I had taken the path upward and eastward. The visibility was dreadful, with a thick, darkening, low cloud shrouding all. The path ascended to finally reach the Bealach na Sgairne at around 400 metres above sea level. It was then that I walked through the curtain of the dark cloud's edge to see unfolding the stunning beauty of Glen Affric and far beyond, with the most perfect and unblemished of blue skies. Left behind were the shades of greyness, the colourless landscape and my limited vision; there before me the distant reach of land in vibrant colour and light. It was good to walk on.

Maybe all 'daybreak' moments are a reminder of history's greatest drama; like Post-it notes affixed to the heart and mind, 'daybreak' moments ever awaken us to a deeper knowing and a greater hope. For we have been told how the Son, on leaving the imprisoning of his cave-tomb, walked into the morning light at the sun's rising, alive and transformed in newness of life. By faith we journey and walk to that 'daybreak' of the Son's making. And we surely sing as we come to this promised new creation, where we will no longer find a landscape with any dying, mourning, crying or pain.

It is good to walk on!

PRAYER

Lord, we thank you for the caves in our lives,
The breakpoints that offer refuge and retreat,
Respite to pierce the tension of flight or fright,
Solace of deep night, calm of wilderness,
A breathing pause from the passing storm
Or the clamour of struggle.
Lord, here we seek the mercy of your shadowing wings,
A steadying of the heart
As faith lifts its eyes
To you, God, exalted above the skies
And in glory over all the earth.

*

Grace notes shall echo in these caves
As in grace you stretch faithfulness over us like the sky
And in love stitch our lives into heaven.

Praise shall rise, the gathering song
Of those restored in the recessed places,
Heartened by your call
From darkness into light,
From the cave to the spacious place,
From the tomb to the garden.
The glory of sunrise, the woken sun,
Honours your name
And calls out our journey
From death into new life,
Towards the dawn.

CHAPTER 13: Sheltering Wings

Those who live in the Highlands have long referred, in Gaelic, to the golden eagle as *Iolaire Dhubh*, or even occasionally in the past as *An t'Eun Mòr*. This great bird has always been a synonym for strength yet also noted for its remarkable gracefulness in flight. What would our lonely Highland glens be like without the high-soaring eagle?

My encounter with the eagle in all its majesty and beauty took place one February day while walking along the high ridge of the Mamores between Am Bodach and Stob Ban. On that polar-cold day, with deep snow covering the hills, an eagle, from far below in the hollow of a corrie, soared upward.

The Mamores in winter

For the briefest of moments this great bird seemed to be almost within my reach. I scrambled hurriedly with gloved hands to pull a camera out of my rucksack for this once-in-a-lifetime photo, only for the bird to continue soaring ever higher, far into the deepest blue of the heavens.

The flight of a soaring eagle inspires in the Jewish midrash[5] a redeeming narrative of how we can be lifted high and brought close to the glory of God, freed from all earthly oppression, conflict, sorrow and weariness. This dynamic imagery is illustrative of God's saving reach to humankind, with his promise of a lasting relationship that is secure through every tempest and storm.

Safe places are greatly valued today. In Psalm 36 the writer associates a longing for refuge with the provision of a safe place under *the shadow* (or *in the shelter) of your (God's) wings*. The imagery of the eagle's powerful and outstretched wings offers an assurance of strength, protection and comfort. The *Sheltering Wings* are a gentle reminder of God's gracious invitation to come home to him and enjoy his loving presence.

> Your love, Lord, reaches to the heavens, your faithfulness to the skies.
> Your righteousness is like the highest mountains, your justice like the great
> deep.
> You, Lord, preserve both people and animals.
> How priceless is your unfailing love, O God!
> People take refuge in the shadow of your wings.
> They feast in the abundance of your house;
> you give them drink from your river of delights.
> For with you is the fountain of life; in your light we see light.
> (Psalm 36:5–9)

Superlatives abound in these words as he measures out the enormous 'wingspan'

---

5. Midrash is the Jewish commentary of the Hebrew scriptures. This particular reference applies to Exodus 19:4 and God's rescue of his people from captivity in Egypt.

of God's love, faithfulness, righteousness and justice – a description of the immeasurable goodness of God so deserving of our trust. This reminder of the dependable character of God becomes in itself the invitation whereby all can come in faith and find their security in his Sheltering Wings. This initiates a lifestyle that embraces new rhythms of grace – ways of living that are both distinctive and quite contrary to the tired and worn patterns of life that once had been so misguidedly endorsed. In his Sheltering Wings, having come to the Father, we acquaint ourselves with his extravagant goodness – blessed with his abundance, his power to refresh and his wise discernment. Through this relationship with God we find security, because now we know who we are, why we live and where this life must lead. This is a great message.

But this message seems less easily heard today, as 'not doing God' has become the default position in so many people's lives. There has been a progressive marginalising of God in our culture along with the diminishing influence of the Christian faith. Has this decline presented new challenges for the well-being of individuals and of our society at large?

One concern that has become more evident in the twenty-first century is the increase in anxiety and fear experienced in people's lives. This is the thesis of an eminent British sociologist, Frank Furedi.[xxxv] If this is true, the immediacy of social media and global issues, such as climate change and the COVID-19 pandemic, has contributed to this trend. However, Furedi's thesis provides a more searching analysis of cultural change. He links a growing fear culture to the loss of an overriding moral authority that once shaped, held and influenced communal life. This is an intriguing thesis.

At the beginning of the twentieth century, Thomas Hardy wrote his well-known poem "God's Funeral", reflecting with some sadness on the demise of Judeo-Christian religion in the UK and Europe and asked, *And who or what shall fill his place?*[xxxvi] A valid question to ask. If God has been erased from the marketplace and the minds of people, then who or what shall fill his place? Accepting Furedi's thesis, this empty space left by the decline in 'God belief' would suggest a serious loss in moral authority, along with a concomitant increase in the anxieties and fears that trouble us in these early decades of the 21st century.

Safety and security are instinctive needs in all our lives, and the psalm writer's Sheltering Wings is indicative of our need for refuge and protection. For the psalm writer, to ask Hardy's question would have been inconceivable. His experience of God would make absurd any thought of the possibility of God's non-existence. Equally, the psalm writer would have had no doubt that moral authority was invested in God, his character and his Word.

If today we are engaging with a society that is more easily troubled by anxiety and fear, then believers have much to offer. We remember how the Son transformed a fearful storm on the Sea of Galilee by calming the wildest waves and the strongest of winds. We live this drama. We live a gospel message that loudly celebrates the Father's gift of peace that stretches beyond all measure. We open this hope to all; there is a peace that can face, overcome and transform the wildest of fears.

But a final word on *Iolaire Dhubh*, that great bird noted for its skill of flight, especially in the days of late autumn and winter storms. A friend once invited me to join him in his search for an eagle's nest somewhere north of Glasgow. My friend had been given the guaranteed six-figure grid reference of its location. We had a great time scrambling about a hillside with map in hand but found no trace of the nest. It may simply have been a one-digit error in the supposedly accurate grid reference that led to our failure but I confess I wasn't too disappointed, being unsure about causing any disturbance to the home of the King of Birds.

The eagle's nest is large and often found high up among the crags of the mountain slope. It's built with branches, grasses, moss, bits of cranberry and other bits and pieces picked up from far and wide.[xxxvii] The *Sheltering Wings* of the eagle provide a caring home for their young through the many weeks of spring and early summer.

And it's these *Sheltering Wings* that depict a most tender image of the caring love of God and his welcoming invitation to come home and find that peace that passes all understanding.

And to come home to God and discover how the illusions of a once ill-constructed life must be gathered up and discarded for good.

To come home and embrace the Father's work of grace that pares, cuts and smooths.

To come home and learn how to bless, to risk, to hope, to stand, to cry, to dance, to love, and more – to learn to fly!

PRAYER

Sheltering God, we rest in the shadow of your wings,
In the mercy of soft down, shielded,
Defended by strength of pinion feather,
We find refuge which calms fear,
The place of protection where your heart's beating
Pulses peace, and steadies our own
To the rhythms of courage.

Nurturing God, with mother heart,
You stir us from the nest and hover,
Watching over our tumbling flight.
You spread the power of your wingspan
And catch our fall,
For you have stooped from heaven's height
To the low place of grace, forever underneath.
Your strong shoulders carry us,
Unweary, unfaint,
In flight, risen on the soaring wings of hope.

CHAPTER 14: Final Thoughts

I recently belonged to a church that had a different approach to the normal congregational weekend away. Our church community went on journeys. Over a long early summer weekend we would cycle and walk across Scotland, from Inverie on the west coast to Inverbervie beside the North Sea – a journey of more than 150 miles. Of course, not everyone did the cycling or the walking, and in fact most of us were part of the extensive support group. Those journeys brought with them times of joy, laughter, small hardships and occasional setbacks. Everyone had to muck in each night at some new hostel accommodation across the width of Highland Scotland, and for a few days we shared as a community, ever growing in our appreciation of each other's worth and value.

Those were good journeys to make and, despite the variable weather, we found delight in the unique attractiveness of Highland Scotland – a scenic attractiveness, not of the kind that could ever claim to be listed in the world's 'top ten' places of outstanding beauty. That list would easily be filled with the Niagara Falls, the Grand Canyon, the Jungfraujoch, the Himalayas as seen from Kathmandu, and other much-visited locations. In Scotland it's not that kind of dramatic beauty, but rather an attractiveness arising out of the intensity and intimacy of many landscapes crammed together on a land area of small proportions. This creates a distinctive kind of beauty.

We must also add the significance of the land's nearness to a great ocean. This proximity allows wind and rain, sun and cloud to dapple the hill and valley with changing colour, shade and light. You revisit the same location again and again, convinced you are seeing the landscape as if for the first time. It brings alive a kind of beauty that is never settled and persistently prompts our sense of surprise and wonder.

On our church journeys we began with the jagged wildness of the west coast, then quickly walked beside Knoydart's rocky and awkwardly shaped mountains. We passed along Loch Laggan and Loch Arkaig. We crossed the Great Glen, with imperious Ben Nevis as a sentinel to all routes east, west, north and south. We circumvented the high round-topped Cairngorms. We admired the beauty of the valleys of the Spey, the Feshie and the Dee. We crossed the high pass of the Cairn o' Mount, eventually descending into lowland Scotland. All of this on a journey of only 150 miles. A landscape of many landscapes, blended creatively to unfold before us the ever-changing beauty that is our Scottish Highlands.

We understand our landscape to have been shaped and sculpted by the force of glacial ice, by timeless weathering and through past disruptions of geological change. Yet astonishingly, in this randomness of creativity of hill and glen, we see also a testimony to the One who first spoke and made and loved. The poet G. M. Hopkins aptly wrote *the world is charged with the grandeur of God*.[xxxviii] And so we are unsurprised that the ancient words and imagery of the psalmist break through upon our land like the angled rays of the brightest sun, revealing the majesty and splendour of God.

So we see God as the Mighty Rock, ever present since the beginning of time. We know his Spirit that flows like a river, awakening in us the blessing of grace. We gaze upon God in his indescribable beauty and, in seeing the sway of the trees and hearing the sea resound, our praise is sung. We are led by God to the spacious place and hear his invitation to come home to the high corries, finding the shelter of his wings. And to bless us on our journey, every new sunrise is his word of hope, bringing the gift of a new day dawning. How extraordinary that as the psalmist's ancient words become re-imagined through our seeing of landscape and land, we embrace a 'grandeur' whose splendour and glory is revealed in God.

But, of course, the Psalms are also deeply personal, addressing the unevenness of our own journey through life. It is Athanasius, a fourth century bishop of the church, who is reputed to have commented that the value of the

Psalms is in the way that "the words speak for us".[xxxix] As we journey we sing and laugh, but we also weep and cry. We know the pit, the cave, the silence, and the danger of the fast-flowing river. The psalmist's "words speak for us", and we own his lament for ourselves. We challenge God to remember his commitment to justice and compassion. We speak and question and even shout against the times of his silence. And yet, in this psalm book of so many thousands of words, what is never lost, even in the darkest of times, is the promise of hope assuring us that on making the journey, the mountain will be reached.

Fiscavaig is not far from the Talisker Distillery on the Isle of Skye. It is an area of land that was resettled in 1923 by sixty families, most of whom came from Harris. This was a good outcome of the Land Settlement (Scotland) Act of 1919. A few years ago I visited some of the homes as their 'stand-in' pastor. On one visit an older lady recalled how, when she was young, on summer Sunday evenings the singing of the Gaelic Psalms would drift across the uneven land of patchwork fields and scattered croft houses. Listening to her, I could imagine how the stillness of the summer evening came alive with this 'music of God', at one with the beauty of creation all around.

In writing this book I have been grateful to those, like my friend in Fiscavaig, who have willingly shared precious memories of times when the Gaelic language was inseparable from a simpler way of life. I understand how the Gaelic Psalms were integral to worship and to an individual's faith. Of course, I've also been aware of the less pleasant realities of these past times: the many occasions of scarcity and hardship, as well as the disappointment of church division.

But much has changed, and the times when the sound of psalm worship wafted gently over the land are long gone. The Gaelic singing of the ancient words has become increasingly rare, and younger precentors of worship are harder to find. The arrival of much-needed incomers to the Highlands and Islands has brought new influences and different patterns of life. My appeal is quite straightforward: it is to encourage new and creative ways of helping others re-engage with the psalmist's message in the 21st century. For in today's landscape of cultural change, our journeys are still characterised by the unchanging themes of hope, despair, betrayal, forgiveness, injustice, celebration and homecoming. Such experiences are integral to life. In the Psalms, these experiences find meaning and spiritual significance in the light of God's glory, power, grace and mercy. Of course, there is always a sadness when what seems special is lost in the cultural identity of a people, but what is never lost is that wistfulness for the eternal that awaits to be aroused and stirred by God's Spirit.

However, I must make one final comment about our church journeys across Scotland. On the Monday of our travels we, cyclists and walkers, finally arrived at Inverbervie, and there were great celebrations. Family members of those making the journey were there to hug and cheer. It was a brilliant moment as we arrived by bike in small groups of twos and threes. However, I do remember it being one of those grey, cloud-filled and raw afternoons on Scotland's east coast. There was no blue sky to match our celebration. Worse still was the unrealised expectation of a celebratory fish supper from the Bervie Chipper. How we had looked forward to that! But to our consternation and disappointment the fish and chip shop was closed.

At Journey's End there will indeed be great celebration. But God does all things perfectly: no grey skies, and certainly no closures of the fish and chip shops! And then we will sing, with grace notes of our own, that new song of lasting praise.

Appendix A

Location of Places

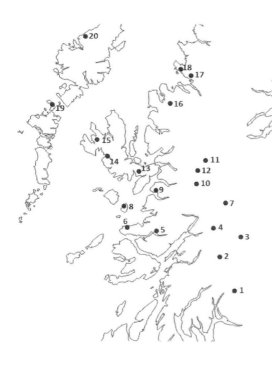

1	Kinlochard
2	River Orchy
3	Clach Cridhe (Rannoch Moor)
4	Mamores
5	Loch Sunart
6	Kilmory
7	Creag Meagaidh
8	Eigg
9	Inverie
10	Glen Kingie
11	Glen Affric
12	Beinn Fhionlaidh
13	Cuillin Ridge
14	Fiscavaig and Portnalong
15	Dunvegan
16	Fisherfield Forest
17	Ben More Coigath
18	Summer Isles and Achitibuie
19	Berneray
20	Barvas

Appendix B

Copyright of Images

Page 17 *Loch Sunart, Ardnamurchan,* © "Still Morning on Loch Sunart" by Odd Wellies is licensed with CC BY 4.0.

Page 24 *Aurora Borealis in the Northern Sky,* © "Belated St. Patrick's" by C. Hollingsworth is licensed with CC BY 4.0.

Page 26 *Cuillin Ridge,* © "Cuillin ridge" by Cathy Whitfield is licensed with CC BY-SA 4.0.

Page 33 *Poor visibility on a mountain path,* © "Back into the mist" by Paul Albertella is licensed with CC BY 4.0.

Page 39 *Summer Isles,* © David Clark.

Page 44 *River Orchy,* © "Easan Dubha, Glen Orchy" by Philip Halling is licensed with CC BY-SA 4.0.

Page 48 *Ben More Coigath from Ardmair,* © "Ardmair Beach" by Andrew Urquhart is licensed with CC BY-SA 4.0.

Page 51 *Clach Cridhe,* © David Clark.

Page 55 *Glen Kingie,* © Kinley Farmer

Page 61 *West Coast, Berneray,* © David Clark.

Page 69 *Fisherfield wilderness,* © "Fisherfield 5/09 (ed74)" by Ted and Jen is licensed with CC BY 4.0.

Page 74 *Old Man of Storr,* Skye, © "World End" by Sanshiro Kubota is licensed with CC BY 4.0.

Page 81 *A Highland dawn,* © "Sunrise-lit mountains and reflections" by Masa Sakano is licensed with CC BY-SA 4.0.

Page 85 *The Mamores in winter,* © "Glen Nevis" by wfmillar is licensed with CC BY SA 2.0

Licences by Creative Commons can be viewed at:

https://creativecommons.org/licenses/BY-SA/4.0/,creativecommons.org/licenses/BY-SA/2.0/, https://creativecommons.org/licenses/by4.0/

Bibliography

N Afrin. *A Critical Analysis of the 1949-1953 Lewis Revival*. MRes thesis, 2018.

W Brueggemann. *The Message of the Psalms*. Augsburg Publishing House, Minneapolis, 1984.

N Campbell. *Reading the Line*. Booklet published in Stornoway, 2005.

F Darling. *Island Years, Island Farm*. Pan Books Ltd, London, 1973.

T Devine. *The Great Highland Famine*. J Donald, Edinburgh, 2004.

F Furedi. *How Fear Works: Culture of Fear in the 21st Century*. Bloomsbury Continuum, London, 2018.

J Goldingay. *Songs from a Strange Land*. Inter-Varsity Press, Leicester, 1978.

S Gordon. *Hebridean Memories*. Neil Wilson, Glasgow, 1995 [Cassell, London/New York, 1923].

S Gordon. *Hill Birds of Scotland*. E. Arnold, London, 1915.

D Gregory. *The History of the Western Highlands and Isles of Scotland*. Hamilton, Adams, and Co., Glasgow, 1881.

J Hunter. *The Making of the Crofting Community*. Birlinn, Edinburgh, 2010.

N MacCaig. *Between Mountains and Sea: Poems from Assynt*. Polygon, Edinburgh, 2018.

J MacKay. *The Church in the Highlands*. Hodder and Stoughton Ltd, London, 1914.

A MacLean. *Night Falls on Ardnamurchan*. Birlinn, Edinburgh, 2001.

D MacLeod. *Memoirs of Norman MacLeod*. Daldy, Isbister and Co, London, 1876.

D MacLeod. *The Living Past*. Acair, Stornoway, 2006.

A Motyer. *Journey*. Inter-Varsity Press, Nottingham. 2009.

E Peterson. *Where Your Treasure Is*. Wm. B. Eerdmans Publishing Company, Grand Rapids, 1993.

D Rixson. *Knoydart – A History*. Birlinn, Edinburgh, 1999.

J Prebble. *The Highland Clearances*. Penguin, Harmondsworth, 1969.

St Giles Lectures: *The Scottish Church*. W. and R. Chambers, Edinburgh, 1881.

D Willis. *The Story of Crofting in Scotland*. John Donald, Edinburgh, 1991.

Prayers that conclude each chapter are by Katy Emslie-Smith

Endnotes

i   Donald MacLeod. *Memoir of Norman MacLeod*. Daldy, Isbister & Co., 1876, p.338.

ii   Gerard Manley Hopkins. *Poems and Prose*. Penguin, London. p. 27.

iii   Norman MacCaig. *Between Mountain and Sea: Poems from Assynt*. Polygon, Edinburgh, 2018, p. 69.

iv   Eugene Peterson. *The Journey*. Marshall Pickering, London, 1995, p. 25.

v   Friedrich Nietzsche. *Beyond Good and Evil*. trans. H. Zimmern, London, 1907, pp. 106–109.

vi   Peter Drummond and Ian Mitchell. *The First Munroist*, The Ernest Press, 1993.

vii   Psalm 119:176.

viii   Psalm 139:13

ix   See Psalms 16:10, 49:15, 71:20.

x   Psalm 40:2.

xi   Robert Burns. 'The Humble Petition of Bruar Water', in W. S. Douglas (ed). *The Works of Robert Burns*. W. Paterson, Edinburgh, 1877.

xii   Psalm 78:15–16.

xiii   Psalm 46:4.

xiv   Psalm 126:4.

xv   Psalm 61:2.

xvi   Psalms 10:1, 28:1, 22:1.

xvii   Psalm 43:2. For details of the Highland Clearances, see John Prebble. *The Highland Clearances*. Penguin Books, Middlesex, 1969, p. 290.

xviii C. S. Lewis. *A Grief Observed*. Faber, London, 1961, pp. 6.

xix   1 Kings 19:12 (King James Version).

xx   Donald MacLeod. *Memoir of Norman MacLeod*. p. 158.

xxi   Exodus 20:3–5.

xxii   Annie Dillard. *The Abundance*. Canongate Books, Edinburgh, 2016. p. 257.

xxiii Psalms 78:14–16, 52-54, 106:13–21, 136:16.

xxiv Psalms 54 and 57.

xxv   For the rationale behind this expression, see Rob H. Marrs and H. A Macallister. *Effects of Long-Term Removal of Sheep Grazing on the Seedbanks of High-Level Grasslands and Blanket Bogs.* Proceedings of National Institute of Ecology of the Republic of Korea, 2020. 1(1), pp. 22–30.

xxvi   Psalm 27:4.

xxvii   Psalm 143:6.

xxviii TS Eliot. *Selected Poems.* Faber, London. p. 77.

xxix   John Muir. *My First Summer in the Sierra.* Houghton Mifflin, Boston, 1911, p. 110.

xxx   Psalm 65:1–4.

xxxi   Galatians 5:22–23 (MSG). Eugene Peterson. *The Message.* Navpress, 2002.

xxxii   Alastair McIntosh. *Island Spirituality: Spiritual Values of Lewis and Harris.* The Islands Book Trust, 2013, pp. 96–97.

xxxiii 1 Samuel 22:1–2.

xxxiv   2 Samuel 23:4.

xxxv   Frank Furedi. *How Fear Works: Culture of Fear in the Twenty-First Century,* Bloomsbury, London, 2018.

xxxvi   A. N. Wilson. *God's Funeral.* John Murray, London, 1999. See Preface.

xxxvii Seton Gordon. *Hill Birds of Scotland.* E. Arnold, London, 1915. p. 16.

xxxviii Gerard Manley Hopkins. 'God's Grandeur', in Christopher Hurford. *The Anthology of Popular Verse.* Parragon, Bristol, 1995. p. 475.

xxxix   John Goldingay. *Songs from a Strange Land.* Inter-Varsity Press, Leicester, 1978. p.17.